"For 150 years the Civil Service Commissioners have played an invaluable role in the work of the civil service. This collection is a fitting tribute which also makes a significant contribution to the important and continuing debate about the future of Britain's public services"
Jonathan Baume, General Secretary, FDA

"Over 150 years the civil service has grown to become one of Britain's great institutions, respected all over the World. This remarkable collection of essays gives a unique insight into the struggles of today's civil service as it seeks to cope with changing and often conflicting demands, while holding fast to the key values of integrity and impartiality"
Sue Cameron, writer and broadcaster

"This collection of essays provides a concise and revealing discussion of the substantial changes now affecting the civil service. No one – politician, journalist or academic – should express an opinion about Whitehall before having read it"
Peter Riddell, Chief Political Commentator, The Times

"The challenge for every generation of civil servants is to adapt to changing times and meet the needs of successive governments while remaining true to the civil service's enduring values. This challenge is as demanding today as it has ever been, and these essays are a fascinating analysis – full of insights – of why this is so. The Civil Service Commissioners play a key role in meeting the challenge, and have characteristically taken the initiative in preparing the book. It is essential reading for everyone interested in the future of the civil service"
Lord Wilson of Dinton
(Cabinet Secretary and Head of the Civil Service 1998-2002)

"It is more customary to receive presents on your birthday than to give them. But by bringing together this collection of essays by people within the civil service and outside observers, the Civil Service Commissioners have provided valuable material for all those interested in assessing how changes in our society are impacting on the profession which supports our government and public services. This collection of essays will be an interesting snapshot to review on the Commissioners' 200th birthday in 50 years' time"

Lord Butler of Brockwell

(Cabinet Secretary and Head of the Civil Service 1988-1998)

CHANGING **TIMES**

Leading perspectives on the
Civil Service in the 21st Century
and its enduring values

Acknowledgements

We owe a debt of gratitude to all the contributors for taking time from their busy schedules to write their essays and for delivering them on time.

A particular thank you goes to Gerard Lemos for his overall contribution and for editing the essays. Special thanks also go to James Anoom and Barry Forrester for coordinating the project and for ensuring its successful completion.

Bill Emmott

Bill Emmott is editor of *The Economist*, the world's leading weekly magazine on current affairs and business.

After studying politics, philosophy and economics at Magdalen College, Oxford, he moved to Nuffield College to do postgraduate research into the French Communist party's spell in government in 1944-47.

Before completing that, however, he joined *The Economist's* Brussels office, writing about EEC affairs and the Benelux countries. In 1982 he became the paper's Economics correspondent in London and the following year moved to Tokyo to cover Japan and South Korea. In mid-1986 he returned to London as Financial Editor; in January 1989 he became Business Affairs Editor, responsible for all the paper's coverage of business, finance and science. He was appointed to his present post in March 1993.

He has written three books on Japan. *The Sun Also Sets: the limits to Japan's economic power* and *Japan's Global Reach: the influence, strategies and weaknesses of Japan's multinational corporations*, were both best-sellers. *Kanryo no Taizai (The bureaucrats' deadly sins)* was published only in Japanese.

In September 1999 he wrote an extended essay for *The Economist* on the 20th century, called Freedom's Journey. In June 2003 he wrote another extended essay for *The Economist*, on America's world role following September 11th, called *Present at the creation*. His new book, which builds in part on the foundation of those essays, is called *20:21 Vision – 20th century lessons for the 21st century*, and was published in February 2003 by Penguin in Britain, Farrar, Strauss and Giroux in the USA and S. Fischer Verlag in Germany.

Foreword

Liberal commentators such as myself are always apt to be suspicious of government in all its forms, from elected politicians to appointed civil servants. Suspicion of power and its motives is in our blood. Indeed, even the most distinguished editor of *The Economist*, Walter Bagehot, author of *The English Constitution* in which he both defined and dignified the role of the monarchy, wrote in the 1860s that: "A bureaucracy is sure to think that its duty is to augment official power, official business, or official members, rather than to leave free the energies of mankind; it overdoes the quantity of government, as well as impairs its quality."

But we also know, or should know, that while an element of such scepticism is healthy when scrutinising any organisation or locus of power (especially the media), to rely solely on scepticism is far from wise and is distinctly unrevealing. In fact it is too easy, an evasion of both truth and responsibility. As Bagehot also wrote, "Nothing can be easier than to make a case, as we may say, against any particular system, by pointing out with emphatic caricature its inevitable miscarriages, and by pointing out nothing else."

During my career (so far) as a writer, judgments of the civil service and of government in general have passed through some wild cycles. Coming as they did after an era in which officials and politicians were thought of as managers of the economy, allocators of assets and pickers of winners, as well as being benevolent and omniscient providers of housing and of safety nets, the 1980s were a period of sharp reaction. Views of government were dominated by Margaret Thatcher and *Yes, Minister*, a time in which all the talk was of rolling back the state and in which the most powerful if superficial image was of civil servants as obstructions to change not agents of it.

That image will never entirely go away, any more than will the idea of businessmen as fat-cats or of journalists as drunkards. But the questions surrounding the civil service have changed, becoming more subtle as well as more wide-ranging. So have attitudes to the role of government: having outgrown the shock of Thatcher and Reagan, the debate is no longer stuck on the sandbank of whether government is good or bad, but has moved on to the far better questions of what sort of government, how it should be motivated, monitored and held accountable, and what exactly it should do. Moreover, another welcome if overdue change is that experts inside and outside government have at last become willing to take note of how things are done in two once seemingly anathema places: the private sector, and abroad.

Every generation tends to believe that they are passing through a period in which change is more rapid, more challenging and more profound than in earlier, more sedentary times. Ours is no exception, and civil servants are as guilty of this narcissism as the rest of us. What is true, however, is that each period of change has its own special characteristics. This anniversary of one of the truly greatest moments of change that the British civil service ever experienced provides a fine opportunity for reflection on what those special characteristics may be.

The essays in this book offer a splendid and thoughtful guide to what those characteristics are. Trust, a word at the heart of the Northcote-Trevelyan reforms of 150 years ago, is one unifying theme: how to preserve it, and the basis for it, as change reaches deep into not only the environment for the civil service but also the very definition of the public sector. Another is the post-Thatcher issue of the appropriate balance between the state and a market economy, between central provision or direction and a free society keen on making its own choices. As the boundaries of the state move backwards and forwards, so the issue of accountability and control becomes more complex, especially given the current interest in outsourcing, private finance initiatives and the like.

There is also an oft-neglected political change which may or not be long-lasting but is certainly important right now in Britain: electoral stability. In the 1960s and 1970s governments changed rapidly, and civil servants offered some continuity, among other things. In the 26 years since 1979 Britain has had only three prime ministers and arguably just two governments: an 18-year Conservative one and (so far) an 8-year Labour one. Such political longevity inevitably alters the relationship between civil servants, ministers and the advisers that surround them, as well, some argue, the relationship between government as a whole and a media which in such circumstances arrogates for itself the role of principal (if disloyal) opposition. And no book can or should ignore the international context for the civil service: that gradually but remorselessly the rest of the world has come to intrude on virtually every action and decision, and certainly on almost every diary. The impact of the European Union is especially great, but there are also many other governmental networks that increasingly impinge. More and more officials spend more and more of their time in contact with their equivalents overseas.

The operations of a great and vast civil service are easy to watch and judge through their specifics but hard to assess and understand as a whole. This anniversary, and this commemorative book, provide an excellent chance to do so.

Bill Emmott

Introduction

The civil service, possibly more than any other institution, has had little guidance as an organisation to shape its development. Since the demise of the Royal Institution of Public Administration there has not been an independent forum for discussion about the civil service.

Reforms particularly since the 1980s have been driven in response to external pressures, perceived dilemmas and political drivers, rather than any continuous systematic assessment of the organisation. The agenda for reform has been predominantly managerial, and much of it has been implemented without much engagement of the public or parliament.

Different aspects of the civil service, that is, its constitutional framework and its capacity as an organisation, have been debated but in isolation from each other. It is welcome that the Public Administration Select Committee has recently embarked on an enquiry into the skills and organisation of the civil service, having done important work on the need for legislation to embed the traditional values of the civil service in legislation.

The Civil Service Commissioners, as custodians of civil service values, operate where operational issues and propriety issues interact. Our experience has convinced us that despite the changes, and perhaps in part because of them, the principles of impartiality and recruitment on merit through fair and open competition remain all the more important. One could argue, "We would say that given our role." So after 150 years, it seemed appropriate to us that we ask others to look into the world of the civil service and throw some light on what they think is at work and how best to reform the civil service and whether the values which underpin it are still relevant.

There is a need to understand the multiple changes that are underway and what their significance is for government, the civil service and its management. These changes are significant and deserve an open debate and not one behind closed doors. The civil service is a national asset: it is held in trust by the government in power for the next administration. We all have a responsibility to ensure that inadvertently no irreparable damage is done to it.

No one doubts that the civil service needs to change and change fast. The questions are what should be the nature of this change; what needs to change and what needs to be preserved.

Anniversaries are a time to look back, reflect and seek inspiration for the future. We hope that this book will encourage reflection, debate and inspire appropriate change.

Usha Prashar

Baroness Usha Prashar CBE

Usha Prashar has been the First Civil Service Commissioner since August 2000. She is also Chancellor of De Montfort University, Chairman of the Royal Commonwealth Society, a Governor of the Ditchley Foundation and a non-executive Director of the ITV.

Previous posts include Executive Chairman of the Parole Board for England and Wales, Director of the National Council for Voluntary Organisations and Director of the Runnymede Trust. She has also held non-executive Directorships with the Energy Saving Trust, Channel 4 and Unite plc.

Her wide portfolio of activities have included membership of the Royal Commission on Criminal Justice, the Lord Chancellor's Advisory Committee on Legal Education and Conduct and the Arts Council. She has also served as Chairman of the National Literacy Trust, as a member of the Management Committee of the King's Fund and as a trustee of the BBC World Service Trust.

She has contributed to a number of publications including *Britain's Black Population* (1980), *Scarman and After* (1984), *Sickle Cell Anaemia, Who Cares? a survey of screening, counselling, training and educational facilities in England* (1985), *Routes or Road Blocks, a study of consultation arrangements between local authorities and local communities* (1985) and *Acheson and After: primary health care in the inner city* (1986).

Usha Prashar was awarded a CBE in 1994 and created a life peer in 1999. She sits in the House of Lords as a crossbencher.

Overview

"The world has changed and the civil service must change with it. The purpose of change: not to alter its ethos and values but, on the contrary, to protect them by making them work in a way more relevant to the modern age."
Tony Blair in a speech given on 24 February 2004 at the Civil Service Reform, Delivery and Values event.

"In the next few years there needs to be a new relationship between the public, parliament, government and the civil service."
Gordon Brown in Anthony Sampson's book: *Who runs this place? The anatomy of Britain revisited* 2004

Introduction

Civil servants today are operating in a very different and fast changing environment. The public has higher expectations than before and is far more demanding. Authority is challenged; inadequate provision is not accepted; litigation over failures is increasing. There has been a growth in external scrutiny. The increase of media outlets and the 24 hour coverage now provided calls for a matching response capacity. Advances in information technology have brought new challenges and vulnerabilities. The public accountability of individual civil servants is increasing steadily. The anonymity of civil servants is eroding.

All this is taking place in an increasingly complex global environment where national borders are becoming less significant and multinational companies are becoming dominant. Political problems are becoming more complex and less predictable. Any attempt to address a problem is subject to the competing advice and opinions of special interest groups, advisory bodies and think-tanks. There is a multiplicity of incompatible perspectives and solutions. This means that outcomes are not always uniform but reflect international, national, regional and local circumstances. Relations with the European Union have to be part of thinking, policy and strategy. Devolution has meant an adjustment in relations between the centre and the devolved administrations. The Freedom of Information Act, human rights legislation and other constitutional changes are making new demands. All these developments challenge the traditional process of policy making and its implementation and delivery.

The focus and intervention of the government has changed. The priorities now are:

- encouraging innovative and efficient private and voluntary sector provision of services purchased by government in areas such as health and social care;
- creating and managing an efficient labour market matching the demand and supply of skills by building the human capital of citizens through education and training rather than using welfare payments as a way of reducing the inequalities between the poor and rich, not just in wealth but also in skills;
- winning markets for products and services and creating an international trade environment in which business can thrive;
- regulating markets to encourage competition and preventing monopoly, exploitation and abuse;
- addressing skills gaps through managed migration;
- containing threats to security and promoting values of democracy; and
- seeking ways of ensuring that increasing cultural and religious diversity combined with a heightened sense of security threats internally does not undermine social cohesion.

Against this background, is the civil service suited to the realities of modern government? Does it have the capacity to meet new demands? Are the current constitutional arrangements still relevant?

The contributors to this collection of essays have emphasised the need for continuous development of the civil service and the complexity and enormity of the organisational and management challenge. At the same time, all have underlined the importance of the enduring values of the civil service. A major reform programme is currently underway, but the push for radical reform began in the 1980s and 1990s. These reforms reflect long standing weaknesses in the civil service some of which were highlighted by the Fulton Report[1] in the late 1960s, which are being exacerbated by the pace of change. Reform now has become a much more conspicuous feature of the civil service and is more comprehensive in scale and scope.

The reforms of the last three decades have aroused concerns that they might undermine or erode the traditional values of the civil service. Publication of the Civil Service Code in 1995 was a testament to this fear. Arguments for a Civil Service Act (first recommended by Northcote and Trevelyan some 150 years ago) have been advanced more forcefully in recent years. Unhelpfully, the debate about the reform of the civil service and a need to ensure the civil service's traditional values in legislation has become polarised. Those who support legislation are seen as traditionalists, not committed to change. Those opposed to legislation are seen as modernisers, committed reformers of the civil service. This is unfortunate because effectiveness of the civil service and its values are intertwined – a point made by Dr Elaine Kamarck, when she argues that in the 21st century, "governments will need to maintain and foster transparency in order to retain public confidence and be held accountable. Here is where democracy and sound public administration come together."

The challenge, therefore, is how to reform the civil service and make it into an organisation which is continually evolving and renewing itself – keeping pace with the changes – while maintaining its values, sense of self-worth and identity. If this challenge is grasped then Sir Hayden Phillips would be right in saying that the "civil service is moving into a period of renaissance."

Civil service and its values

Reasons for reasserting and reiterating the values of the civil service are given by all the contributors, albeit from their different perspectives.

Donald Savoie asserts the significance of the merit principle: "It should be even less necessary today to enter into any lengthened argument to demonstrate the importance of a national civil service than it was 150 years ago. There is ample evidence that countries with a weak civil service have weak economies and widespread corruption in both their public and private sectors. If citizens do not trust their public institutions, society cannot function properly. Northcote-Trevelyan had it right when they prescribed the merit principle to staff the civil service."

Sir Hayden Phillips puts it differently. He says: "The work of government, and therefore, the day to day work of the civil service will continue to be formed out of the rich mixture of winning party manifestos, events, forceful or weaker political and official personalities and, hopefully, a sound bedrock of strong evidence, good argument, and a growing understanding of public expectation.

These relationships and the hectic welter of life in government sustain the enduring values, the cultural folk memory, the sense of belonging to more than one small part of the machine. The civil service will continue to need the values of honesty, integrity, objectivity and impartiality but allied to flexibility, political sensitivity and commitment."

Sir Andrew Turnbull argues that "Every successful organisation has an ethos or culture to sustain and strengthen it. In the civil service the bulwark is a strongly held set of values… These values permeate every part of the civil service. That is a major source of cohesiveness in an essentially federal organisation, and provides a strong base to support the civil service's adaptability… As the organisation and skills of civil servants change a strong commitment to our values is vital."

Gerard Lemos emphasises why there is a need for a permanent civil service in today's world: "Given the long timescales involved and the intractable nature of many of the problems described, it is the permanent civil service, working with and through others… that must change to become the archivist of professional memory, the record-keeper of change, the notator and evaluator of innovation and the begetter of networks and new structures and systems. Above all, the permanent civil service must be the impartial, objective and far-sighted adviser on the financial and other investments needed for a better future."

From an international perspective Dr Elaine Kamarck says, "While the world has made great strides in democratisation in the last three decades that democratisation has often been incomplete. Elections have been held, power has changed hands peacefully but the routine interactions between citizens and their government are still governed by an unchanging ruling class that is all too often plagued by corruption, dishonesty and prejudice. The first world needs to protect the hard won independence and honesty of the civil service tradition and the rest of the world needs to create a civil service that can lead to more just societies."

Civil service reform

The need for urgent reform is undisputed. Sir Andrew Turnbull's and Gus O'Donnell's essays make the direction of travel and the nature of change clear. They both allude to the fact that there is a need to enhance current capabilities like policy advice, human resources, financial and information technology management; but that there is also a need to develop new ones, such as service delivery, project management, working through others, managing relationships with external actors within a framework of appropriate accountability and regulation which promotes learning and does not stifle innovation and creativity.

Although the scale and the scope of the current reform agenda is more comprehensive and coherent, its pace needs to be accelerated. There is also a need to change the culture of the organisation to one which is more outward looking, less risk averse, and designed to encourage learning and to enable others to become involved and influence change. The civil service needs to learn to do things differently, developing a relationship between the centre and other parts of the private, public, and voluntary sector that is not one of control but of mutual learning; where audits and inspections are part of on-going learning; where the parties concerned actively reflect on what they do and how they learn; which facilitates the growth of individuals, organisations and communities. This means laying less stress on claiming to know what is best but putting more emphasis on making the best use of knowledge and learning acquired through partnerships and working through others. In other words not just learning to deliver with and through others but using the experience and knowledge to learn and adapt. Dr Elaine Kamarck underlines this when she says that "as many studies of organisations – both public and private – have shown, innovation tends to come, not from the top people in the organisation but from those in the middle and on the front lines. Thus the best public sector organisations tend to create an atmosphere in which all employees – from top to bottom – feel free to participate and to communicate."

In such a process of policy development and delivery, involvement, legitimacy and accountability become critical. It demands working methods and relationships which are enabling and transparent and where a demarcation of roles is clear. The modern civil service, therefore, needs to learn how to develop meaningful mechanisms for involvement which enhance legitimacy and deliver effective outcomes. It also requires appropriate accountability and regulatory frameworks. Government and the civil service have been grappling with all these issues and a number of steps have been taken to meet new demands, but it is a mixed picture and a number of concerns have been raised by Sir Alan Langlands and Baroness Onora O'Neill. Sir Alan Langlands says, "Yet again this complex management task is being played out against the shifting sands of structural change, a proliferation of new regulatory bodies and a lingering sense of command and control from central government."

Baroness O'Neill draws attention to the fact that the distinction between management and accountability has been blurred. She argues that 'intelligent account' of the nature of the work done by wider public sector institutions needs to be taken into account and that this cannot be done by concentrating on selected indicators of performance devised primarily for management purposes. She goes on: "Intelligent accountability is not a matter of micro-management from afar, but of ensuring informed and independent scrutiny of performance."

Then there is the question of regulation. Dr Elaine Kamarck says, "Regulatory reform is a critical, if imperfectly understood aspect of economic development." The Better Regulation Task Force has been working in this area and the government is now in the process of establishing a Better Regulation Executive whose task will be to reduce unnecessary burdens in both the private and public sectors, and an advisory body comprising of stakeholders whose main function will be to give advice to the executive. The principles which will guide the activity of the executive are proportionality, accountability, consistency, transparency and targeting.

Baroness O'Neill, however, draws attention to the fact that the definition of regulation by the Better Regulation Task Force "as any government measure or intervention that seeks to change the behaviour of individuals or groups" is so generous that many issues and roles are blurred. She rightly says that "a lot of the difficulties faced by the public sector arise from an assumption that since government, and thereby the civil service, fund the public sector and initiate legislation… they must not only hold to account but control and manage its delivery of services." This confusion has led to a consequent blurring of roles and responsibilities and has created as Baroness O'Neill says, "large difficulties for government and for the civil servants. By taking increasing control of the delivery of public services, governments become accountable to the electorate for delivery of those services. Every failure is seen as a case of government failure, of government missing its targets, or failing to improve public services." She points out that, "those who take the blame seek to reduce the problem by constantly altering and adding to the ways in which they control those who actually deliver services.

There is some irony in this outcome."

The need for 'better regulation' and an appropriate regulatory approach is discussed by Sam Younger who warns of a risk of "drowning legitimate activity in bureaucracy and red tape or worse still the state is given overweening power to force conformity with rules that stifle the freedom and enterprise of individuals and of society at large." He goes on to say: "More generally, regulatory bodies must balance their ability to understand the needs and views of the regulated with an ability – however imperfect – to reflect a wider public interest. Independence and impartiality, therefore, have to be balanced by a real understanding of the activities being regulated and a willingness consistently to engage and to listen. Equally, independence has to be balanced by accountability; consistency in the way in which regulation is applied is a key consideration but has to be balanced with a flexibility and a sense of proportionality… Finally, and in many ways the most difficult of all to achieve, is the flexibility and tough mindedness not to assume that the regulatory activity being undertaken now will necessarily be valid for all time. It can and should, though, be the subject of continuous debate and adjustment."

The relationship between ministers and senior civil servants

All these changes are having an impact on the nature of the relationship between ministers and senior civil servants. Donald Savoie describes the changes thus: "By the 1970s and 1980s politicians set out to build a new mega-village, one that would redefine their relations with career officials and the work of the public service. Indeed, they began calling for a different breed of civil servant altogether, one that was much more responsive on policy. In consequence, career officials become uncertain about their policy work. The provision of fearless advice became difficult to sustain once a high degree of responsiveness was demanded by politicians… Civil servants have become reluctant to explain why things must be so, to provide objective, non-partisan advice, and to explain what kind of trade-offs are required if a certain decision is taken, and so on. One former deputy minister in Canada writes that, 'loyalty itself is being redefined as obsequiousness and fawning. The honest public servant is in danger of being superseded by the courtier'."

The Industry Forum in association with the Smith Institute[2] put forward the notion of the 'policy entrepreneur'. They argued that "ministers come to the office primarily concerned with outcomes, desired changes in society which they have been elected to bring about. Pretty soon, they get enmeshed in the detail of how to deliver these outcomes, and all too frequently, put in the position by civil servants when they are required to make decisions not only about what should be delivered, but how it should be delivered and in some detail. There is a defensiveness about the culture of the civil service which places ministers in a position they are ill-equipped to succeed in, and which fails to use the knowledge that civil servants have."

The report goes go on to argue "it is time to break out of the vicious circle. Indeed, if we do not break out of it, there is little chance of meeting the government's objectives. A policy entrepreneur does not try to substitute his or her own objectives for these of elected ministers, and is driven by democratic values that accord strong legitimacy to the electoral process. But a policy entrepreneur does make things happen, overcome obstacles and achieve results, is undaunted   or not much daunted   by the risk of failure, and driven by ambition to succeed in creating the circumstances for achieving outcomes."

They go on, "As that context changes, as systems, structures and processes are changed to enable the new agenda to be achieved, we hope that leadership potential of civil servants as policy entrepreneurs will be allowed to flourish. We have met some policy entrepreneurs in undertaking this research. Long may they flourish and act as role models and mentors to the next generation."

Senior civil servants now do not only have the role of devising policies but also have a role of devising a process for developing policy, managing it effectively to deliver the outcomes. Emphasis is on strategic capacity, policy coordination and effective delivery mechanisms. While top civil servants continue to play a key role between politics and administration, they also now need to be effective managers – putting in place organisation wide systems, balancing in their own work strategic management, financial management and human resource management. Their role now is to ensure that the system of getting advice is one of synthesising advice drawn from multiple sources. They are now leaders operating the machine, managing change and managing the interface with ministers. Gus O'Donnell elaborates this point and argues that, "no single individual is likely to master the range of issues – policy and delivery; specialist and generic – and that therefore the focus for civil service leaders should be on building a strong and balanced team."

The other side of this equation is ministerial responsibility and accountability, but less attention has been paid to this issue. The emphasis has been on the civil service and its management and not the role of ministers. Donald Savoie addresses this issue in his essay when he says, "Politicians, meanwhile, avoided looking to their own institutions or their own role, as they set out to 'fix' government. Career officials, given their anonymity under ministerial responsibility, could not speak out, publicly at least. If they could have, they might well have advised politicians to 'heal thyself' and their institutions before setting out to heal the civil service." He quotes John Major who in 2003 in his book, *The Erosion of Parliamentary Government* warned that all facets of parliamentary government were in grave difficulty. He writes "we have scarcely noticed that the timbers which support it are creaking and diseased, and are in danger of collapse. The structures remain but many of them are hollowed out. The erosion is evident from top to bottom." He detected a change in philosophy in the relationship between ministers and career officials, insisting that "too many ministers behave as if officials should be committed extensions" of the government's electoral reform platform and that from the "Prime Minister downwards politicians openly blame civil servants for errors that have in the past been accepted as the responsibility of ministers – and still should be."

Complex processes of policy making, and diverse ways of delivery combined with the obliteration of significant distinction between management, accountability and regulation, as argued by Baroness O'Neill, have led to blurring of boundaries and responsibilities between ministers, civil servants and the wider public, voluntary and private sectors. This highlights the importance of ensuring that reforms are not just managerial but ones which derive their legitimacy and authority from a democratic mandate. Government has to be effective and efficient but also accountable. Distinctions between management, accountability and regulation along with clear boundaries and rules of engagement are all important. The reform of the civil service, therefore, cannot be looked at in isolation. Operational matters, constitutional issues and democratic mandates are interrelated. Ministerial responsibility and accountability requires revitalisation through the House of Commons, being "the representative intelligence of public concerns from the many and varied constituencies right across the country", as argued by Sir Hayden Phillips. It is for this reason a Civil Service Act is needed. Sir Hayden states: "It would give to parliament, and not just to the government of the day, a different stake in the long term future of the civil service, and provide an outward and visible sign of the link between constituency representation and the relationship the civil service must have through Ministers, to communities up and down the land."

Civil service, media and communication

Changes in the environment within which the civil service operates, changes within the civil service and the trend of public disengagement from formal mechanisms of democracy necessitate new and innovative ways of connecting and engaging with the public. But Baroness O'Neill warns that 'transparency' and 'communication' are different. She argues that, "transparency requires information to be made available – but it does not require that information to be communicated in ways that are accessible to and useful for particular audiences."

John Lloyd in his paper on 'Media and Politics' points out that providing information for the public at large used to be a task for the media. He reminds us that, "in a genuinely free society, media's civic role should rather be to assist the people of that society to understand all kinds of powers – state, corporate, associative, cultural, foreign – so they, the people, can hold them to account through their actions, chief among which must be voting and other participation in civic life."

Baroness O'Neill regrets that, "large parts of the media have abandoned this role, and the contribution to democracy that it makes. When the media do not report systematically to citizens, it is tempting for government to insist that the civil service take over the task. But if they are to take on this task, it cannot be reduced to transparency, any more than holding to account can be conflated with quasi-management from afar."

The government has recently taken steps to raise its game. Howell James in his essay on 'The Age of Explanation' spells out that "government communication should have two overriding objectives: to make the voice of the public heard at the policy table so that government develops and delivers services which better reflect people's expectations and desires; and to improve the public's awareness and understanding of government policies and actions so that people can more readily identify and access information and services relevant to their daily lives. We need to more fully embrace a culture of explanation – where communication informs all stages of the policy making process."

However, the shift towards a communicative and explanatory mode of policy making is taking place against the background of low levels of trust in government, politicians and institutions. If this approach is to work effectively it needs to be based on trust – trust of people in institutions and trust of government in people. The integrity of the process, therefore, is crucial. It is for this reason that Howell James sees the importance of traditional values of the civil service: "if the emphasis is being broadened, the heritage of the values should not change. If there is to be a common currency for debate, information shared and trusted by the public, the media and the political classes, the impartiality of the civil service will need to continue to underpin all government communication activity."

Conclusion

The need for the continuous development of the civil service against the background of constant change is all too evident. New challenges will continue to bring further adjustments and reforms, create new and different relationships between the state and the citizen, between the public, private and voluntary sectors, between management and politics. But it is clear that proper conduct has always been a prerequisite to good governance. The success of reforms and changes and indeed overall confidence in government depends on it. Professor Dennis Thompson of Harvard University sums it up well: "When ethics are in disorder, when citizens reasonably believe they are, one should not be surprised that disputes about ethics drive out discussions about policies. Ethics makes democracy safe for debate on the substance of public policy. That is why it is so important. That is the sense in which it is more important than any other single issue."[3]

Notes

1. The Report of the Committee 1966-1968 on The Civil Service, Cmnd 3638
2. Empowering Government: Reforming the Civil Service, November 1999
3. Paradoxes of Government Ethics, *Public Administration Review*, Vol 52, No 3, May/June 1992

The Changing Context

In *From Quiet Village Life to a World only for the Brave*, Donald Savoie asserts that the collapse of the traditional boundaries and the drive to make the civil service more like the private sector has demolished the unique bargain struck between the civil service and politicians. The luxury of frank and honest debate is at risk.

Sir Hayden Phillips sees the civil service as being in something of a renaissance, arguing that the service is increasingly outward-looking and accepting of shared responsibility. The traditional values of honesty, objectivity, impartiality and integrity all continue but allied with political sensitivity, flexibility and commitment.

Donald Savoie

Donald J. Savoie has degrees in politics and economics and holds the Canada Research Chair in Public Administration and Governance at the Université de Moncton, Canada. He has wide experience in government and academe.

Dr. Savoie has published numerous books and his articles have appeared in the leading journals of political science, public administration and public policy. His work has won prizes in Canada, the United States and France. He was elected Fellow of the Royal Society of Canada (1992) and made an Officer of the Order of Canada (1993). He was awarded the Vanier Gold Medal (1999) for having made a significant contribution in the field of public administration in Canada and the Trudeau prize (2004).

He has also been awarded several honorary doctorates and has been selected as Visiting Fellow at All Souls College, Oxford. His most recent book is *Breaking the Bargain: Public Servants, Ministers, and Parliament*, published at the University of Toronto Press.

From Quiet Village Life to a World only for the Brave

One wonders if Sir Stafford Northcote and Sir Charles Trevelyan could have had any idea of the impact their report – brief, succinct as it was – would have on the workings of government throughout the Western World. Their report codified the values of impartiality, integrity and staffing based on merit that have guided the work of career officials for 150 years in every corner of the world. The Northcote-Trevelyan report also laid the basis for a bargain between politicians and career officials that would shape their relationship and establish an administrative space from which career officials could make decisions relatively free of partisan political considerations. The purpose of this essay is to revisit the Northcote-Trevelyan report, assess its application in today's environment and report on the evolution and current state of the civil service.

Village life

One of the vivid images in Hugh Heclo and Aaron Wildavsky's book, *The Private Government of Public Money* involves "village life in the civil service."[1] The comfortable life in this political-administrative village had a number of characteristics. First, there was mutual respect among the inhabitants, and the civil service was thought of as a partner and, more significantly, as an ally of the political executive. In the Westminster model, the village system tended to be closed, permitting more private negotiations and agreements among the parties involved than in other systems of government. Further, civil servants' political neutrality made the village mentality secretive. Mutual respect was in part a function of a second characteristic of the Westminster model – mutual dependence.

The work of Northcote-Trevelyan made such a village life possible: without it, the civil service would have continued to be a mere extension of the political executive. A distinct administrative space belonging to the civil service was established. The merit principle in staffing civil service positions led to a "bargain" or an understanding between elected and career officials, over their respective duties to guide mutual relations. This traditional bargain has over the years helped shape how power is distributed and controlled in modern society. Under the arrangement, public servants exchanged overt partisanship, some political rights, and a public profile in return for permanent careers, or at least indefinite tenure, anonymity, selection by merit, a regular work week, and the promise of being looked after at the end of a career that did not require paying close attention to their own material self-interest. Politicians, meanwhile, gave up the power to appoint or dismiss public servants and change their working conditions at will, in exchange for professional competence and non-partisan service to the government of the day.[2]

Thus began a golden era for the public service. At the time, there was a widespread belief that government was a positive force for improving the economy and society and both the civil service and individual civil servants were widely respected. Civil servants spent their whole career in the service and, for the most part, stayed with the same department throughout. A well-developed organisational memory assisted their competence. Career stability meant that they would remember a long line of past policies and their fates. The system allowed them to offer unwelcome advice to decision makers when necessary. The tenure and the respect that they enjoyed permitted them to advise a minister that he or she was heading in the wrong direction. That advice was not always heeded, but it was very likely given. In these golden days, trust in government was high and any calls for access to information legislation or protection for whistleblowers lay in the distant future.

The civil service won respect because it was very careful with taxpayers' money. The village led a very frugal existence. Government was considerably smaller than it is today and everything of consequence that involved the spending of public funds was brought to the attention of senior career officials and ministers. There was a time when budget deficits were considered a "great political, and above all, a great moral evil."[3] Gladstone laid down in simple terms the budget process of his day: "New wants are always coming forward, but where… provision is made for those new wants it ought to be counterbalanced by new economies." The way to ensure this, in his view, was to "estimate expenditures liberally, revenue carefully and make each year pay its own expense."[4] The Gladstone view held sway for a long time, and not just in Britain. Former Canadian Prime Minister Lester Pearson became exasperated, as a senior civil servant at Foreign Affairs, at the level of financial details requiring a ministerial signature. He wrote a memorandum in October 1941 to his deputy minister asking how he was "going to show the Prime Minister how to win the war and make the peace if you have to spend two hours each day talking about the cost of Désy's table linen or the salary of the newest stenographer."[5]

In summary, the village that provided a home for civil servants and elected officials was small, accessible, comfortable and financially prudent. Trusted by the public, it constituted an effective mechanism for governing. But things started to change in the 1970s. the village came under fire as the environment of politics, the nature of political leadership and government operations themselves were transformed by the emergence of a new and complex world.

Although the values grounded in the Northcote-Trevelyan report endured, the traditional bargain began to fret away at the edges and village life became no longer tenable. Aaron Wildavsky observed in the mid 1980s that "the most senior bureaucracy is now only for the brave."[6] Today career officials live in several, often competing, villages. Much of their world is in a state of flux. The traditional tenets derived from the Westminster and Whitehall models are being challenged both from within government and by outside forces.

Now only for the brave

In 2003, former British Prime Minister John Major, in *The Erosion of Parliamentary Government* warned that all facets of parliamentary government were in grave difficulty. He writes: "we have scarcely noticed that the timbers which support it are creaking and diseased, and are in danger of collapse. The structures remain but many of them are hollowed out. The erosion is evident from top to bottom."[7] He detected a change in philosophy in the relationship between ministers and career officials, insisting that "too many Ministers behave as if officials should be committed extensions" of the government's electoral platform and that from the "Prime Minister downwards, [politicians] openly blame civil servants for errors that have in the past been accepted as the responsibility of Ministers – and still should be."[8] His observation is hardly limited to Britain. The same has been heard in Canada and Australia.[9]

Public opinion surveys in Anglo-American democracies have also consistently told us that public confidence in government institutions has dropped significantly over the past twenty-five years or so.[10] This decline is due in part to the general decline of deference in society. But there is more at work here. A theoretical challenge to the idea of a career public service as a condition for good government began to emerge in the late 1970s. Public-choice and agency theorists posited that career officials promote their own self interest and that this could well be at odds with the wishes of elected representatives and those whom they represent. In addition, they claimed, career officials, given their secure position, had more influence than politicians and could get their way in establishing government priorities.

The hugely successful BBC television series *Yes, Minister* has a lot to answer for. It was a satire, but some saw it as a documentary. It had a profound impact on how the public service was perceived, not just in Britain but wherever it was seen. A Canadian academic wrote that it became "something of a cult program, exceedingly popular with a small following that is intensely interested in public affairs."[11]

The series painted a portrait of ministers as publicity-seeking dimwits who were no match for the highly educated, unprincipled, and Machiavellian career officials. No matter the issue and however sensible the minister's position, Sir Humphrey, the senior official, would have a position at odds with the minister's and he would invariably prevail. Sir Humphrey's views were rooted in an ideology that stubbornly favoured the status quo and, more important, he would do anything to protect the interests of the department and the public service. Sir Humphrey not only shaped all major policy decisions and ran the department, he also managed political crises on behalf of his hapless minister. No matter the issue, the minister in the end had to rely on Sir Humphrey's considerable political and bureaucratic skills simply to survive.

By the 1970s and 1980s, politicians set out to build a new mega-village, one that would redefine their relations with career officials and the work of the public service. Indeed, they began calling for a different breed of civil servant altogether, one that was much more responsive on policy. In consequence, career officials became uncertain about their policy work.[12] The provision of fearless advice became difficult to sustain once a high degree of responsiveness was demanded by politicians. In the new climate, officials found it prudent to recommend safe policy options, what "politicians would wear." They became wary of saying *'No, Minister'* or even *'Be Careful, Minister.'*[13]

Civil servants have become reluctant to explain why things must be so, to provide objective, non-partisan advice, and to explain what kind of trade-offs are required if a certain decision is taken, and so on. One former deputy minister in Canada writes that "loyalty itself is being redefined as obsequiousness and fawning. The honest public servant is in danger of being superseded by the courtier."[14] One can get a sense of how the policy world inside government has shifted by contrasting the views of two Canadian deputy ministers, one writing in 1961, the other in 1996. Al Johnson, in 1961, insisted that "frank talk" is paramount, even if it may endanger a happy union between the career official and his political chief. He quoted Sir Warren Fisher that "the preservation of integrity, fearlessness, and independent thought and utterance in their private communion with ministers of the experienced officials selected to fill up posts in the service is an essential principle of enlightened government."[15] Contrast this with George Anderson, a deputy minister of Intergovernmental Affairs in the Privy Council Office, writing in 1996: "Overbearing advisers have a way of being cut down to size. The officials with most influence are those who are best attuned to the views and needs of ministers."[16]

Politicians, meanwhile, avoided looking to their own institution or their own role, as they set out to "fix" government. Career officials, given their anonymity under ministerial responsibility, could not speak out, publicly at least. If they could have, they might well have advised politicians to "heal thyself" and their institutions before setting out to heal the civil service.

Policy making also became far more complex, if only because major policy issues could no longer fit neatly into a single department. By the 1970s, cross-cutting policy issues began to surface everywhere so that even traditional line departments could no longer work in relative isolation from other departments or even other levels of government, and new policy measures, however modest, came to involve several departments and central agencies. Issues to do with the environment, trade, and human resources, for example, would affect virtually every government department.

There was also an unprecedented assault on boundaries of all sorts. The assault has been subtle and the changes introduced by stealth, but the impact has been far reaching and profound on the whole machinery of government. Boundaries within government, between governments, between government and the private sector, and between government and citizens are all collapsing. The space in the village which elected and career officials once occupied in relative isolation has been opened, the walls demolished.

Hierarchical organisation, departmentalisation, division of labour, specialisation, division of responsibility, specific responsibilities assigned to every position in the form of job descriptions, all these are designed to establish organisational boundaries. Boundaries serve many purposes. They establish who has legitimate access to certain decision-making arenas, as well as departmental mandates and who is responsible for what. They enable those at senior levels to exercise control and to hold subordinates to account for their decisions and activities.

Government agencies and departments have historically been organised in a defined hierarchy of offices with clear lines of authority. John Stuart Mill argued over 125 years ago in his *Representative Government* that responsibility is best provided and the work best done if all functions of similar subject be allocated to single departments.[17] However, this practice that once guided the development of our machinery of government no longer holds. Now each department or agency comes to the table with only part of the answer in hand, unable on its own to impose a comprehensive solution. In brief, policy issues no longer respect organisational boundaries and, as a result, policy-making has now become horizontal, consultative and porous. In Britain, the term "joined-up" government and in Canada the term "horizontal government" are the new fashion and they have come to permeate virtually every document that comes out to central agency.[18]

The impact of e-government on government operations and the delivery of services is well documented.[19] Less obvious is the impact it is having on policy development. What we do know is that e-government is already making vast quantities of information available to citizens, interest groups, think-tanks and research institutes. This alone should introduce a new dynamic to the policy-making process. A number of people have remarked on the enormous potential of e-government, suggesting that moving from the industrial age to the information age will transform the nature of democracy.[20] British Prime Minister Tony Blair has said that the present era has the potential to be "the second age of democracy."[21]

It is already becoming clear that governments have less control over who knows what and when, and a new networking model is emerging that does not conform to the old command-and-control departmental model. The internet is opening up government everywhere to scrutiny on a scale never seen before.[22] Mel Cappe, former Secretary to the Cabinet in Canada, spoke to this when he observed that "e-government requires public servants without borders, people who can work effectively across departments, programs and other borders … who see an issue in a broader, horizontal context."[23] He had earlier written in his annual report that "e-Government is about people: new skill sets, mindsets and leadership approaches. It will transform how public servants work, relate to each other, do business, and engage citizens and other partners." Because of e-government, he said, the government was "moving away from a traditional model of public service based on hierarchical, directive management."[24]

New information systems are horizontal by design and capable of penetrating all sorts of boundaries in government. Information flows not only between departments but also between government and outsiders, and that in itself tends to dissolve boundaries. This, in turn, makes it difficult to operate a hierarchical model because one simply cannot control cyberspace.[25]

Access to information legislation is also breaking down boundaries between governments and their citizens. The media now can ferret out snippets of information and uncover political and administrative foul-ups and miscues. Though the legislation is making government more transparent in one sense, it has also made career officials reluctant to commit their views and recommendations to paper. The fear is that these could surface in the media and force officials to support or defend them in public or embarrass their ministers. This, in turn, flies in the face of the traditional role of career officials in the Westminster model, since the views and advice of civil servants are to be private and their actions anonymous. One senior Treasury Board Secretariat official in Canada recently admitted, "We are now all sitting ducks. I cringe when I write an e-mail because I never know whether it will appear on the front page of a newspaper six months down the road. It is possible now for someone to ask for all exchanges, including e-mails, between senior official X and senior official Y.

We can no longer blue-sky or have a playful mind. We no longer have the luxury of engaging in a frank and honest debate. It is now very difficult to put down on paper – Be careful, minister, there are problems with your ideas and what you want to do."[26] One can assume that this leads to less disciplined thinking, as carefully worded memoranda are replaced by Powerpoint presentations. Ironically, because it is no longer committed to paper, the advice to "be careful," if given at all, has become less transparent.

Governments have also been busy trying to break down organisational boundaries that separate the public from the private sector to make the former resemble the latter. There was a time when career officials saw a great deal of merit in red tape, due process, and valued its distinguishing features from the private sector. Forty years ago a senior career official could stress the importance of a "slow and meticulous" process in the "recruitment of staff."[27] No senior civil servant would claim this today. Indeed, they now speak about the need to become task-oriented and to look to "clients" for guidance rather than to the world of institutions and historically derived processes and identities. Many speak disparagingly of the dead hand of bureaucracy which they would like to invigorate with a management concept inspired by the private sector. By the 1990s, virtually every government department in the Anglo-American democracies were using phrases borrowed from the business vocabulary in all their planning documents. It seems that anything to do with government could and should be re-stated from a business perspective. Moreover, the search has been on for years in all Anglo-American democracies for public-private partnership models that would leave the "rowing" to the private sector.[28] It has become accepted wisdom that management in the private sector is invariably superior to that found in government, conveniently overlooking the fact that the two sectors are vastly different and that the public sector mostly operates under processes and rules that would not be tolerated in private business.

Regional trade agreements (NAFTA, in the case of North America), the emergence of market states and supra national institutions have also transformed nation states and their governments. Globalisation is much more than a catchphrase. At a minimum, there has been a pooling of sovereignty in alliances, enabling policies to be struck and decisions to be made to move the global economy. This is true not only with respect to trade policies and practices, but also to a host of other policy fields, especially monetary policy. The policy levers once available to national governments to control the flow and mobility of capital are less and less available or, if they are, the price to be paid to manipulate them is prohibitive. It can be argued, for example, that Reagan's 1981 tax cuts initiated a worldwide shift to lower corporate and income taxes and the consequences are still being felt today. Firms and even individuals have access to highly sophisticated means of communication, and they respond quickly to higher levels of taxation, new labour laws, or tougher pollution legislation. In addition, in recent years the world banking community has become increasingly "deregulated" and "decartelised."[29] There is also strong pressure to harmonise a wide variety of laws and policies from one nation state to another. Robert Reich brought this point home when he wrote that the well-being of Americans depends on the value that they can add to the global economy and no longer only on the profitability of their own corporations.[30]

Hand in hand with globalisation, we are seeing a shift towards an American-style rights-oriented society.[31] The application of the charter of rights in Canada and repeated calls for bills of rights for Britain and Europe are evidence of this. It is important to remember that those who put forward claims under a charter or a bill of rights do so under the "most powerful of all moral considerations" and are in no mood to compromise.[32] This movement is happening at a time when historically marginalised groups, such as visible minorities and religious groups, are gaining prominence on the political agenda. They want straight answers to their grievances and they will seek truth in the courts rather than in the less clear-cut world of politics and civil service. This politically focused cultural pluralism has given rise to radically different types of cleavages in society, putting still more new pressures on the structures of government.

All of the above pose new challenges for the concept of civil service accountability in that blame avoidance may well now be the easier path to pursue. It is becoming clear that we are moving away from Max Weber's classical model in which the individual bureaucrat is not allowed to "squirm out of the apparatus in which he was harnessed… He is chained to his activity by his entire material and ideal existence."[33] Public servants can now squirm out of the apparatus in which they are harnessed because there are different harnesses available to them, most of which are porous, and they are strongly encouraged to establish new partnerships with non-government groups. Governing by emulating the private sector is, however, fraught with problems. We have plunged headlong into empowering public sector managers so that ministers and senior career officials no longer need to be concerned about such things as the cost of Désy's table linen. However, we never figured how to assess properly the performance of mid-level public sector managers and hold them to account for their management decisions. New Public Management initiatives served to diffuse systems of accountability in government precisely at a time when virtually everyone outside of government was clamouring for stronger accountability.

Dealing with the new world

The past thirty years have played havoc with virtually all aspects of public administration. The pace of change and the nature of the change are such that one is tempted to echo Wildavsky and write that public service is now only for the brave and simply leave it at that. After all, the changes are not fully in place and there is every indication that still more are on the horizon.

That said, there are a number of things that remain constant. Northcote-Trevelyan wrote 150 years ago: "It cannot be necessary to enter into any lengthened argument for the purpose of showing the high importance of the Permanent Civil Service of the country in the present day. The great and increasing accumulation of public business and the consequent pressure on the

Government need only be alluded to. It may safely be asserted that… the Government of the country could not be carried on without the aid of an efficient body of permanent officers, occupying a position duly subordinate to that of the Ministers who are directly responsible to the Crown and to Parliament, yet possessing sufficient independence, character, ability, and experience to be able to advise, assist, and, to some extent, influence, those who are from time to time set over them." It should be even less necessary today to enter into any lengthened argument to demonstrate the importance of a national civil service than it was 150 years ago. There is ample evidence that countries with a weak civil service have weak economies and widespread corruption in both their public and private sectors. If citizens do not trust their public institutions, society cannot function properly. Northcote-Trevelyan had it right when they prescribed the merit principle to staff the civil service.

If anything ails national civil services, it is those who never tire of trying to make the public sector look like the private sector. Democratic organisations are in the first instance organisations intended to foster democratic representation and accountability, as an end in itself. It is for this reason that due process, fairness, lengthy deliberations, red tape, and the keeping of records are all-important in government.

Civil servants in the years ahead will continue to see their machinery of government re-invented to make government operations more efficient, to make horizontal or joined-up government work better and to generate stronger policy advice. Civil servants need to be present in these efforts. However, they need to double their efforts to establish the value of their work to society, to demonstrate the impact of their programmes and to show in concrete terms what taxpayers are receiving for their taxes. This is something that matters greatly to our increasingly sceptical society. There is a widely held perception that the civil service, as an institution, has abandoned its frugal ways. In brief, in the rush to emulate the private sector, the civil service may well have lost sight of its most important defining characteristic – its ability to husband public funds in an efficient manner.

It appears that in the shift from "administration" to "management" career officials became less careful with public money. Embracing private sector ways without the discipline of the market to establish performance leads to spending with less accountability. Preaching better management by looking at how the private sector operates does not establish standards that have to be met.

There are things, however, that should remain constant for, if they do not, national civil services will be in peril and society will be poorly served. These include the merit principle, the ability to give frank and fearless advice to elected officials, the integrity and political impartiality of civil servants. The Northcote and Trevelyan report served society, history and government well for 150 years and there is every reason to hope that it can continue to serve us as well for the next 150 years.

Notes

1. Hugh Heclo and Aaron Wildavsky, *The Private Government of Public Money* (London: Macmillan Press, 1981).

2. B. Schaffer, *The Administrative Factor* (London: Frank Cass, 1973).

3. Quoted in Aaron Wildavsky, *How to Limit Government Spending, or...* (Berkeley: University of California Press, 1979), p. 169.

4. Ibid., p. 173.

5. John Hilliker, *Canada's Department of External Affairs: The Early Years*, vol. 1 (Montreal and Kingston: McGill-Queen's University Press, 1990), p. 243.

6. Quoted in Christopher Pollitt, *Managerialism and the Public Service: The Anglo-American Experience* (Oxford: Basil Blackwell, 1988), p. 97.

7. John Major, *The Erosion of Parliamentary Government* (London: Centre for Policy Studies, 2003), p. 1.

8. Ibid., pp. 9–10.

9. See, Donald J. Savoie, *Breaking the Bargain: Public Servants, Minister, and Parliament* (Toronto: University of Toronto Press, 2003) and Michael Keating et al., *Institutions on the Edge?* (St. Leonards, Australia: Allen and Unwin, 2000).

10. See Joseph S. Nye Jr., "Introduction: The Decline of Confidence in Government," in Nye et al., eds., *Why People Don't Trust Government* (Cambridge, Mass.: Harvard University Press, 1997), pp. 1–2.

11. Sandford F. Borins, "Public Choice: Yes Minister Made It Popular, But Does Winning the Nobel Prize Make It True?," *Canadian Public Administration*, vol. 33, no. 1 (Spring 1988), p. 22.

12. See, among others, Donald J. Savoie, *Thatcher, Regan, and Mulroney: In Search of a New Bureaucracy* (Pittsburgh: University of Pittsburgh Press, 1994).

13. Ibid., p. 341.

14. B. Ostry, "Making Deals: The Public Official as Politician," in John W. Langford, ed., *Fear and Ferment: Public Sector Management Today* (Toronto: Institute of Public Administration of Canada, 1987), p. 171.

15. Johnson, "The role of the deputy minister: III," *Canadian Public Administration*, vol. 4, no. 4 (1961), p. 373.

16. George Anderson, "The New Focus on the Policy Capacity of the Federal Government: I," *Canadian Public Administration*, vol. 39, no. 4 (Winter 1996), p. 471.

17. John Stuart Mill, *Considerations on Representative Government* (New York: Harper, 1869), p. 100.

18. See, for example, "Wiring it up: Whitehall's Management of Cross-Cutting Policies and Services," London: Performance and Innovation Unit, Cabinet Office, 2000).

19. See, for example, Ignace Snellen, "Public Service in an Information Society," in B. Guy Peters and Donald J. Savoie, eds., *Governance in the Twenty-first Century: Revitalizing the Public Service* (Montreal and Kingston: McGill-Queen's University Press, 2001), pp. 297-343.

20. See, among others, Reg Alcock and Donald G. Lenihan, *Opening the E-Government File: Governing in the 21st Century* (Ottawa: Centre for Collaborative Government, 2001), p. 8.

21. Quoted in Joseph S. Nye Jr., "Navigation in the Internet Age," *John F. Kennedy School of Government*, Op Ed [web site] (Cambridge, Mass.: President and Fellows of Harvard College, 2004), at **http://www.ksg-harvard.edu/news/opeds/2000/nye_internet_ft.htm** and Darin Barney, *Prometheus Wired: The Hope for Democracy in the Age of Network Democracy* (Chicago: University of Chicago Press, 2000), p. 21.

22. See, for example, "Caught in the Net," *The Economist*, 24 March 2001, p. 26.

23. Mel Cappe, "Remarks to the Arthur Kroeger College of Public Affairs, Leadership Forum Awards Dinner," Ottawa, Privy Council Office, 6 February 2002, p. 7.

24. Mel Cappe, *Eighth Annual Report to the Prime Minister on the Public Service of Canada* (Ottawa: Privy Council Office, 2001), p. 3.

25. Quoted in Barney, *Prometheus Wired*, p. 238.

26. Ralph Heintzman, quoted in Donald J. Savoie, "Searching for Accountability in a Government Without Boundaries," Canadian Public Administration, vol. 47, no. 2 (Spring 2004), p. 17.

27. David Osborne and Ted Gaebler, *Reinventing Government: How the Entrepreneurial Spirit is Transforming the Public Sector From Schoolhouse to State House, City Hall to Pentagon* (Reading, Mass.: Addison-Wesley, 1992).

28. Johnson, "The role of the deputy minister: III., p. 373.

29. See, for example, *The Economist*, "A Survey of Multinational," 27 March 1993 and "A Survey of International Banking," 10 April, 1993.

30. Robert B. Reich, *The Work of Nations* (New York: Alfred A. Knopf, 1991).

31. Allen C. Cairns, *Charter Versus Federalism* (Montreal: McGill-Queen's University Press, 1992).

32. Tom Parklington, "Against Inflating Human Rights," *The Windsor Yearbook of Access to Justice* (Windsor, On.: University of Windsor, 1982).

33. Quoted in Louis C. Gawthrop, *Public Service and Democracy: Ethical Imperatives for the 21st Century* (New York: Chatham House Publishers, 1998), p. 11.

Sir Hayden Phillips GCB

Sir Hayden Phillips is Chairman of the National Theatre, Senior Advisor at Hanson Capital Ltd, and Charities Consultant to HRH The Prince of Wales. He is a Director of St Just Farms Ltd, of De Facto 1119 Ltd, and is on the Advisory Board of Englefield Capital. He is also a member of the Councils of Marlborough College and of Salisbury Cathedral, a Trustee of the Fitzwilliam Museum Cambridge, and an Honorary Bencher of the Inner Temple.

His previous career was in the Civil Service. He was Permanent Secretary of the Department for Constitutional Affairs (formerly the Lord Chancellor's Department) from 1998 to July 2004, and Permanent Secretary of the Department for Culture, Media and Sport (formerly the Department of National Heritage) from 1992 to 1998. Before that he held senior posts in the Treasury (1988 to 1992), the Cabinet Office (1986 to 1988), the Home Office (1974 to 1976 and 1979 to 1986), and in the Office of the President of the Commission of the European Communities (1977 to 1979). From 2002 to 2004 he was Permanent Secretary with special responsibility for the Honours system and his review of the system was published in July 2004.

He was educated at Cambridge (Clare College) and Yale.

Why on Earth would you join the Civil Service in the 21st Century?

Prelude: The summer of 1967

I joined the civil service in July 1967. Entering the gloomy portals of the Home Office, opposite the Cenotaph on a brilliantly sunny day, with my long hair shortened at my father's insistence, I reported to the Principal Establishment Officer: pinstripe trousers, black jacket, bowler hat on the peg (him not me). There were two of us fast-streamers starting that day and he told us that there were two available postings, one in police research and development and the other in burials, cremations and exhumations. Did either of us have a strong preference, he asked?

These were still quite well mannered days and as each of us, lying, denied any preference, he proposed tossing a coin to decide our allocation or, as I keenly felt, my whole future career and happiness. He extracted the coin from his pocket and prepared…and then my new colleague burst out that he had a preference. My thoughts about him at that moment were neither collegiate nor printable. He said "I would really like to work in burials, cremations and exhumations."

And so, to my relieved delight, my civil service career began. Looking back what was it like?

In retrospect the most extraordinary thing was the internal class distinction. I had joined the Administrative Class whose members were paid to think (because they had demonstrated that they were clever), to advise ministers on policy (which is, on the whole, why they had joined), and to write elegant prose. The Executive Class was separate. They mostly had not had the privilege of a university (then mostly Oxbridge) education but they managed the vast majority of civil servants, delivered services (in current jargon) and supported "us". With rare exceptions the ambitions of members of the Executive Class could only be limited.

This arrangement was of its time. 1967 was only five years after the Gentlemen played the Players at Lords for the last time, each team having not only separate dressing rooms but separate entrances onto the field.

The training given, to all the year's entry cohort, in Regent's Park was excellent and fun. There was however, no sense then that our pathway of development would take us into management. We were there for the honing of intellectual and analytical skills, the mastery of governmental and parliamentary process, and the quick learning of a genuine, if temporary, expertise in our subject area.

Compared to today it felt a very enclosed world. There were no special advisers; and few think-tanks. Interchange with the private sector or the wider public sector was extremely rare. This sense of joining a religious order as a trainee direct entry bishop was strongly reinforced on one occasion when I suggested to the head of my division that I should visit a police force which was enthusiastic for one of the projects I was working on. His reply: "I wouldn't do that if I were you. It will prevent you from being properly detached."

Money seemed to grow on trees as running costs were automatically increased for inflation. Government did not yet quite live in a 24 hour media world. There seemed more time to think about what was the right step to take. The coverage of parliament in the written press was extensive, and serious.

Indeed, one of the strongest memories of my early life in the Home Office, was the priority given to the quality of the drafting of answers to parliamentary questions. The process was totally hierarchical: only a Head of Division could formally submit a reply and it then moved through the Assistant Under Secretary of State, the Deputy Under Secretary of State, and then the Permanent Under Secretary. This style of working was quite common more generally. The constant second guessing this involved, not necessarily of substance, but certainly of form, was de-motivating; but the succinct quality of language and the sense of priority to be given through ministers to parliament were immensely valuable and I tried to hang on to those values throughout my career as the nature of what we did and the culture in which we did it were transformed.

So where are we now?

Opinion polls on the public's level of trust make depressing reading if you are a senior civil servant but worse still, in descending order, if you are a Labour Minister, the Chief Executive of a large company, a Conservative politician, an estate agent, or, worst of all, a "tabloid" journalist. These judgements about trust have varied little over the last twenty years. If you want to be highly trusted in your professional life you should choose to be a family doctor, school teacher or local police officer.

There is interesting paradox in relation to the civil service as a part of public service. Despite a continuing disengagement from traditional party politics (the 1997 election briefly excepted) and a continuing series of critical stories in the press about the processes of politics and government, there has been a real revival of interest in the civil service as a vibrant component of public service.

Applications to join the civil service fast stream have recently been at an all time high. Of course, those who apply will have various motives. For some it will be a form of job insurance; a few may apply because they don't know what else to do; but for most it is because of a genuine interest in the business of politics and government, and of finding work in which you could really try to make a difference.

In a lecture he gave last year, the playwright, David Hare, precisely defined for me a central strand of public service motivation, although in the context of the theatre: "If I am to try to understand the strange jumpy figure in the beige rib-knit pullover and the white drainpipe jeans, smoking 40 a day and grabbing every Marx Brothers film he could find, then I would say I had already begun the task of trying to resolve certain impossible confusions which still haunt me. You want the world to be different. You want injustice to be addressed. You want a social system which relieves the ubiquitous suffering of the poor. Why on earth do you imagine that theatre might be an effective, even an appropriate, way of achieving such things?"

Indeed, if you want to make a difference why on earth would you join the civil service in the 21st Century?

In 1967 the high importance and critical relevance of the civil service was assumed. Over the last thirty years we have moved from that position through a period in which the civil service became not only less fashionable but also, for some, a form of public service which was actively unhelpful to the national interest compared to the private sector. Now there is a revival of its importance, not because its centrality is assumed in the way it was before, but because it is winning a new positive reputation. The civil service is, I believe, moving into a period of renaissance.

The world is now in Whitehall

Work in the civil service has become, and will increasingly become, more international so that there will be few parts of government which can form policy and implement it with a purely domestic focus. This is not only the result of our membership of the European Union, although that is crucially important. It is surprising how long it took, in many parts of government, for the relevance of our entry in 1973 to sink in, no doubt reflecting the disabling British schizophrenia about Europe which regularly infects public opinion, politicians and the press.

But the contribution which the United Kingdom will be able to make goes well beyond the confines of an enlarged European Union, not only in terms of economic policy but on environmental issues, on national and international security, and on justice, both civil and criminal. As Permanent Secretary of the Department of Constitutional Affairs I was able to see, at first hand, the value placed by other countries – in Eastern Europe, China, Russia, Africa, India – on judicial and legal cooperation. In the next twenty years the UK's international standing can be enhanced by the contribution we make in fields well beyond foreign, economic, and international development policy. All ministers and civil servants will have to make more space to enhance the British contribution to global issues. This is something which the Foreign Office warmly encourages, although they still have to struggle to persuade some domestic departments of its value to the United Kingdom.

The way we work

This process of reaching out rather than looking in is becoming, and must increasingly become, the way civil servants need to work inside government. Forming and reforming multi-disciplinary teams is becoming the way in which new strategies are prepared and implemented and the delivery of public services sharpened. This isn't easy to do or to sustain. The natural tendency of all corporate bureaucracies, whether in the private or public sector, is to revert to the comfort blanket of silo working. Weaning people away from the settled clarity of hierarchical line management where everyone thinks they know precisely where they stand and can more directly bolster their sense of status and self-esteem by being able to say "this is my responsibility not yours" is a constant struggle.

To sustain a new culture of cross-boundary working, especially across hitherto separate departmental and ministerial responsibilities, will require constant vigilance, vision, and indeed a new and different sharing in success or failure, especially because the thrust of delegation from central controls, and the executive agency creation programme, the major change of the 1990s, reinforced the "this is mine" approach. "This is ours" is a much harder message to embed than it sounds. It is easily destroyed by political rivalry, departmental jealousy, and simply a loss of energy.

The way the civil service deals with the public and indeed its own staff needs constant thought and attention, as does the balance between flexible discretion to help individual citizens, and fair and equitable treatment of all.

When my late step-father-in-law, Mark Bonham Carter, was Chairman of the Race Relations Board he asked the Board Secretary if he could have a pencil sharpener. He was told he could not as his consumption of pencils was insufficient. The Secretary said that his hands were tied by the rules. This relationship between volume and sharpness was clearly invented by someone who did not live in the real world.

The point of this story is a reminder that, despite the enabling capacity of modern technology, the risk of excessive regulation and bureaucracy is a chronic problem, and it may be further increased if technology encourages treating real people in a mechanistic rather than a human way. Greater openness and responsiveness need to become the hallmark of the way government departments work.

The new professionalism

These changes still have some way to go to be sustainable but should be reinforced by a third strand of contextual change, namely the push for increasing professionalism in all strands of civil service work. This is not about old arguments around generalists and specialists, nor more recent ones about administrators or managers, but about professional skills and knowledge in all aspects of work. It has now really begun, perhaps belatedly, in financial management, human resources, procurement and estates management.

The changing ecology of the civil service both reflects and engenders professionalism. People join with experience of business, banking, education, local government, the NHS, and take up central and not peripheral roles. The mix of cultures that results is invigorating, and supplies a process of constant learning and renewal.

The transformation is not yet complete but the new plan for three broad families of skills in the civil service – policy development and the management of government business, the management of operational businesses, and corporate services – provides for a much more coherent approach for bringing forward a better range and balance of skills for senior posts than the civil service has had in the past. The proviso has to be that this will only work if the best talents get good experience in each of these areas, and that there is genuinely parity of esteem.

How decisions are made matters

The changing context will affect the way decisions are made and communicated, especially in relation to the delivery of public services. There is, it is said, much greater trust and acceptance of decisions made locally, and that moving power and accountability outwards and downwards from Whitehall and Westminster is therefore critically important. This presents a difficult dilemma for any government. Does it seek, in the face of that pressure of demand, to bolster existing local institutions, despite the fact that local government, in a famous phrase, seems to "stir up apathy", or since public services are delivered through many different processes of accountability, does it tailor new mechanisms for engaging community interest?

Despite the rhetoric of localism, change can sometimes in fact be effectively driven from the centre, not because Whitehall knows best but because national government has the power and resources to make things happen. The risk is a too oppressive weight of performance targets and reporting systems which sap the energy and blunt the motivation of those who have to do the work at the sharp end.

There is no 'best' answer to this dilemma, other than that ministers and civil servants should continuously focus on ways in which public expectation and satisfaction about how decisions are made can be regularly tested. In that process perhaps a revised role for parliament can be found. Not in the sense of the House of Commons as a party political cockpit but in its being the representative intelligence of public concerns from the many and varied constituencies right across the country. I hope that is not too old-fashioned a thought.

Constitutional change and open government

The fifth strand of contextual change which will require fresh thought and present some unforeseeable challenges is the relationship between constitutional changes, accountability and openness.

The constitutional landscape is surprisingly different from a decade ago. The Freedom of Information Act is part of a largely unremarked on (save by the cognoscenti in academia, in the broadsheet press, and in the House of Lords) period of massive constitutional reform. These changes – devolution, the creation of London government, the unimagined variety of new voting systems for different elections, human rights legislation, and a new concordat between the Executive and the Judiciary – have yet to show their full impact. That will probably take two decades. These changes both respond to, and then fuel in turn, greater public expectations for consultation and openness. The civil service as well as politicians will need to think through carefully how that pressure is handled alongside the demand for faster and faster decision making under an intense media spotlight.

In this changing context civil servants and ministers must hold on to the capacity to pause for thought, and to say that they are doing so, and not be driven into an e-mail culture of instant reply. As my former boss and mentor Roy Jenkins put it when we were debating Freedom of Information proposals in 1975, ministers must retain the right "to change their minds in private".

There is one more brick to be put in the wall of constitutional change and that is a Civil Service Act. This essay is not the place to reflect on the valued flexibility of prerogative powers and Orders in Council versus the virtues of an Act. There will also be differences of view about what such an Act should cover. I favour a legislative base for the civil service for two simple reasons:

a. if we believe that the rapidity and demands of change will persist then it must be sensible explicitly to recognise in law the fundamental principles of selection and promotion on merit, and the political impartiality of the civil service; and

b. it would give to parliament, and not just to the government of the day, a different stake in the long term future of the civil service, and provide an outward and visible sign of the link between constituency representation (to which I referred earlier) and the relationship the civil service must have through ministers, to communities up and down the land.

So what endures

The work of government, and therefore, the day to day work of the civil service will continue to be formed out of the rich mixture of winning party manifestos, events, forceful or weaker political and official personalities and, hopefully, a sound bedrock of strong evidence, good argument, and a growing understanding of public expectation.

These relationships and the hectic welter of life in government sustain the enduring values, the cultural folk memory, the sense of belonging to more than one small part of the machine. The civil service will continue to need the values of honesty, integrity, objectivity and impartiality but allied to flexibility, political sensitivity and commitment.

Anthony Howard writing in *The Times* on 19th January 2005 said: "For better or worse, flexibility and detachment are these days at a discount, while commitment and convictions are valued at premium rates."

I hope he is not right, but he and others are right to warn, certainly as far as the policy advice function is concerned. But commentators should also remember that the vast majority of people in the civil service are engaged in trying to manage and deliver better public services, and commitment is of higher value than detachment in that endeavour.

As the pace and complexity of change grow the civil service needs more leadership than when change was slower and the sense of embedded tradition deeper. Each new generation of civil service leaders needs to impart to each incoming cohort in a way that did not seem necessary in the past what the right balance is between enduring values and changing demands. And that has to be done visibly, frequently, and persuasively.

On three or four occasions a year I took part in a discussion group for new entrant, fast-stream civil servants. Over the years the topical content changed but invariably four issues used to come up on each occasion: relations between ministers and officials, especially at the top; politicisation; career development; and could they, as individuals, make a difference.

I would explain that it was important to escape from the brilliant caricature of *Yes, Minister*, of manipulative civil servants and stupid ministers, or its antithesis of overbearing ministers and supine civil servants. The important issue, as in all organisations that depend on teamwork for success, was building good personal relationships. Working with ministers, or for them with civil servants, was like living in a series of arranged marriages which could be immensely strong and successful if both sides worked honestly and openly at the relationship. Politicisation of civil servants had not been my experience but that, as in any walk of life, each side of the relationship preferred to work with people whom they liked. That was human nature, not politicisation.

As to careers, then and in the future, success and the achievement of ambition would lie in being both mandarin and manager but as I have explained the new plans for development are now more coherent and sophisticated than implied by that shorthand reply. And the civil service will increasingly look for and get a more diverse intake of people – social background, ethnic origin, professional experience – throughout a career lifetime but without the automatic expectation of a lifetime career.

Will the new generations of civil servants be able, as individuals, to make a difference to the real world, given the sheer scale and complexity of work in government? My reply for the future remains the same as it has in the past; of course they will, indeed why else would they have joined.

CHANGING **TIMES**

The Implications for the Civil Service of the Changing Context

In *Continuity and Change* Sir Andrew Turnbull looks at the development of the civil service against the backdrop of rapid global and technological change. The focus on delivery has created a greater demand for leadership and professionalism.

Sir Andrew Turnbull KCB

Sir Andrew Turnbull was appointed as Secretary of the Cabinet and Head of the Home Civil Service on 2 September 2002.

Sir Andrew read economics at Cambridge and in 1968 went as Overseas Development Institute Fellow to work as an economist for the Zambian Government. He joined HM Treasury in 1970 where apart from a secondment to the IMF in 1976–78, he remained until 1983. Between 1983–85 he was Private Secretary (Economic) to the Prime Minister and in 1988 returned to Number 10 as Principal Private Secretary, returning to the Treasury in 1992. Sir Andrew was Permanent Secretary to HM Treasury, 1998–2002, and before that Permanent Secretary to Department of Environment/Department of Environment, Transport and the Regions, 1994–1998.

In addition to his formal role, Sir Andrew is also the Chairman of the Civil Service Sports Council and Commodore of the Civil Service Sailing Association.

Continuity and Change

One of the defining characteristics of the environment in which the civil service, and indeed any other large organisation, currently operates is change. In many ways the current world of the civil service would be unrecognisable to Sir Burke Trend, Cabinet Secretary when I joined the civil service in 1970. Paradoxically, at the same time the nature of the changes that we need to adapt to, and the aims of the current reform programme are also characterised by continuity. This paradox is important to understand in considering the reform programme.

Drivers of change

Three key changes are of the most relevance to the civil service in the twenty-first century.

i. Problems are increasingly complex, in large part because of globalisation. The problems and issues faced by any country, including the UK, can no longer be isolated from the rest of the world. The events of 9/11 and its aftermath show this conclusively. Economic policy has now to be made with an eye to the state of the economies of countries across the globe. The growth in the Indian and Chinese economies has enormous impact for the services and industries in the UK.

ii. At the same time, as levels of wealth and information have expanded, expectations about the quality of public services have risen accordingly. People are no longer prepared to accept monolithic service provision based on the principle that the service provider knows best. In an age where customers can access their bank or utility provider 24 hours a day, they expect, and deserve, a more personalised response to their healthcare (as Alan Langlands argues elsewhere in this collection) or education needs. The huge increase in the availability of information means customers can compare the service they receive.

iii. The explosion in communications media has had a huge effect too. Citizens can access far more information, much more quickly and cheaply than has been possible before. The provision of information has seen massive diversification – anyone with access to the internet can rapidly pass information to large numbers of other people. Multiple media channels operate 24 hours a day reporting events almost as they happen. Governments are expected to respond on the same basis. Many parts of the media no longer function as media but as players with their own agenda. This has promoted a culture of cynicism. Many of these developments are not new. The Fulton report on the civil service of the mid-60s noted changes which required adaptation from the civil service – notably technological change and vast amounts of new knowledge, a corresponding increase in the complexity of problems and solutions, an increase in the international nature of the setting of government work resulting from improved communications and the greater interdependence of nations.

What is new is the scale and pace of change and the way that organisations are expected to respond to it. The revolution in information and communication technology is a case in point. In 1970, about the same time as I became a civil servant, the first microprocessor was invented, paving the way for widely available personal computers and, ultimately the creation of access to the internet for millions of people. Twenty years later many civil servants still didn't have a computer on their desk, and the vast majority of correspondence was carried out by paper even as recently as 1997. Today even 5 year olds use computers and access the internet, and it's rare to see a minute distributed in hard copy only. Change has become continuous, rather than stepped. In response to this, organisations seek continually to measure their abilities against the external environment and build and develop their capacity in response.

The developments in the external environment described above require two responses from the civil service. First, the civil service needs to adapt to the challenge of using new technologies, to the new information requirements resulting from 24 hour media and so forth, to continue to be an effective organisation. Second, the civil service has to support the way that the government has chosen to respond to societal changes with its programme of public service reform. One could devote a whole book to describing and analysing this programme, but in brief the aim is to deliver services which are focused on the needs of the user, rather than the provider, and which include a much greater element of choice than before. The civil service needs to respond to this agenda by building up its capacity to develop and deliver this programme.

However, as highlighted above, although we need to change some of what we do, and the way that we do it in response, we can also rely on a certain amount of continuity. A look back at the historical precedent illustrates this well.

Change in the civil service

The first great reform of the civil service took place following the Northcote-Trevelyan report in 1854. The report set out the fundamental purpose of the civil service, and although we have come a long way in the last 150 years, their description is still a valuable one – as Donald Savoie notes in his earlier essay.

"The great and increasing accumulation of public business, and the consequent pressure upon the government, need only be alluded to; and the inconveniences which are inseparable from the frequent changes which take place in the responsible administration are matter of sufficient notoriety. It may be safely asserted that, as matters now stand, the government of the country could not be carried on without the aid of an efficient body of permanent officers, occupying a position duly subordinate to that of ministers who are directly responsible to the Crown and to parliament, yet possessing sufficient independence, character, ability and experiences to be able to advise, assist, and to some extent, influence, those who are from time to time set over them."

Northcote and Trevelyan's civil servants were primarily focused on administration and policy advice. Over a hundred years later, between 1966 and 1968 a committee chaired by Lord Fulton returned to the question of the fitness for purpose of the civil service. The committee addressed the question of the primary functions of civil servants, concluding that these were the development of policy, running of government business and, "operating policies embodied in existing legislation and implementing policy decisions – for instance through managing and controlling major programmes such as the design of Polaris installations".

How much has this changed? Some tasks remain the same, at least in outline, and some civil servants are engaged in functions that would be familiar to Fulton's committee, or indeed to Northcote and Trevelyan. Ministers still need support from civil servants in running government business – replies to parliamentary questions still need to be drafted, legislation still needs to be drafted and guided through parliament. The provision of policy advice is still an important function, though the civil service no longer has a monopoly.

But alongside this continuity, there are significant changes. Most importantly, our most important functions include not just advising but also doing. Our focus is no longer on managing plans and services according to the legislation, but on developing high quality public services that meet the needs of the public. We no longer expect to develop policy from the centre and have little hand in its delivery.

I would identify four key functions for the civil service today:

- Developing creative and strategic policies
- Designing and delivering services directly or in partnership which meet the needs of the public
- Using public money efficiently
- Upholding our core respected values of integrity, impartiality, honesty and objectivity.

Policy making

This is an area of continuity, but it is also one of substantial change. The changing environment has produced, as well as an increasingly complicated set of problems to tackle, an ever more complex map of stakeholders, of whom the most important are perhaps customers. This affects the way policy advice is produced in many ways, but I would pick out one particular development: the way strategies and policies are developed.

In the old model, civil servants embedded in policy directorates produced strategies on those policies. Increasingly we are seeing a new approach, where strategy is made off-line. In some cases this is still carried out within departments, though more and more within dedicated strategy functions. In others, particularly where there is a cross-cutting element, this happens in the centrally based Strategy Unit, bringing together departmental officials with representatives of stakeholders and external experts. We have also seen the emergence of clear departmental strategies and five-year plans, setting out the core role of the department, alongside a cohesive set of policies to achieve this. This is part of a wider movement, discussed below, ensuring that departments are clearly focused on priorities, and are clear about who does what.

The design and delivery of services

Delivery of services by civil servants is nothing new. Civil servants have been administering benefits, issuing licences and permits and rescuing those in difficulty at sea, amongst other things, for a long time. But the way we think about, and approach, this task has changed in several ways:

i. We no longer see this as the poor relation of policy advice – we recognise that service delivery is one of the most important things we do.

ii. We increasingly see ourselves as operating in partnership with others in the wider public sector (and in some cases the private and voluntary sectors) to deliver services like education and healthcare.

One of the most notable results of the introduction of Public Service

Agreements in 1998 was that departments became formally responsible, for the first time, for outputs in the wider public sector, and thus for leadership of those sections of public services. More recently, departments have been taking a long hard look at themselves and what they do to answer questions about whether they are providing the right sort of leadership to those delivering services, whether the chains stretching from the department to the front line are too long, and whether the balance of resources is in the right place. In most cases, the result has been a slimming down of departmental headquarters. Some of the resulting headcount reductions have resulted from efficiencies being made. In other cases, they result from a recognition that some functions are best placed closer to the front line.

Efficiency

The efficiency imperative is not new; there have been a number of initiatives before – most notably the Financial Management Initiative in the 1980s. This time, however, the parameters are different, and provide a focus for one of the key issues in the debate on public services. In the 1980s, the debate was centred around whether services should be run by the public sector or the private sector, with the argument based on a crude dichotomy of 'private sector good, public sector bad'. In the 1990s a new phase of the debate began. By the latter part of the last decade questions were being raised about whether services were improving and who was best placed to deliver them. The issue of choice was also being raised. A more sophisticated phase of the debate is now underway in which the question is broadly, are the results of public sector reform justified by the amount of money being spent on them?

The government has sought to answer this question through two complementary initiatives.

i. The Atkinson Review has sought to find better ways of measuring public sector outputs, and productivity, so that it's clearer what we're getting for the money.

ii. The Gershon Review aimed to ensure that money was better spent, and to change the ratio of spending between the centre and the front line, with the latter getting a higher share. Gershon identified a number of areas where efficiencies could be made – for instance through better procurement, more efficient transactional services and shared corporate functions. The actions being taken to meet the review's recommendations will have far reaching effects on the way the civil service works.

Values

The final function is the maintenance of our traditional values. Every successful organisation has an ethos or culture to sustain and strengthen it. In the civil service the bulwark is a strongly held set of values – of integrity, impartiality, honesty and objectivity. These values have been upheld for a long time – even a report as critical as Northcote-Trevelyan noted that 'the trustworthiness of the entire body is unimpeached'.

These values permeate every part of the civil service. That is a major source of cohesiveness in an essentially federal organisation, and provides a strong base to support the civil service's adaptability. A strong political consensus supports a politically impartial civil service. As the organisation and skills of civil servants change a strong commitment to our values is vital. In this the civil service has the support both of parliament and the Civil Service Commissioners. A Bill has been drafted which seeks to emphasise these values while allowing the civil service to be managed flexibly.

Implications for civil servants

These changes have a number of substantial implications for the careers and skills of civil servants. The first is leadership, and with this greater visibility. Traditionally the civil service has not seen strong leadership as an important skill, for three reasons.

- First, civil servants share leadership with ministers, who have ultimate control over the agenda.

- Second, this is a collective endeavour with the wider public sector.
- Finally, it is claimed that so many factors affect public sector outputs, so the impact of leadership from any one organisation is difficult to isolate.

The focus on delivery creates both a demand for greater leadership, and the opportunity to exercise it. In particular, the civil service has a new relationship with the wider public sector. Rather than thinking of the civil service as a discrete section of the public service, civil servants are essentially one part of the chain stretching from ministers to those delivering services on the front line. In this conception of the civil service, headquarters departments act as the leader of the relevant wider public service – so for instance the department for Education and Skills is seen as the leader of the education system.

This means senior civil servants taking on a different role to that of the traditional faceless bureaucrat (though this image has been in decline for some time). It means much more visibility and a new set of characteristics. The new generation of leaders in the civil service need to take personal responsibility for delivering results effectively and swiftly and to work across traditional boundaries, to be focused on strategic outcomes, honest, realistic with staff and ministers, and to constantly seek to update their learning and development.

This agenda for change also calls for the killing off once and for all of the concept of the generalist. In truth we moved away from this a long time ago. More professional skills are now being embedded into the civil service, primarily through being clear about the career paths people are expected to follow. The skills to support the government to deliver better public services cluster around three families – corporate services, operational delivery and policy. These families include specialists like accountants and economists.

In future, therefore, civil servants' career paths need to focus primarily on one of these three areas, though those reaching the most senior levels will be expected to have experience of all three. The result should be that the corporate services are much more professional than Whitehall has traditionally had.

Equally the operational delivery skills that many private sector organisations have had for years will be present in the civil service. In particular, the civil service needs to improve its ability to deliver projects and programmes – though contrary to the media portrayal of Whitehall procurement and project management we already have a large number of successes under our belt.

A fourth, and related, key plank of the response to change is a commitment to bring in and develop talent so that the civil service better reflects the society we serve. Northcote-Trevelyan were able to recommend: "Our opinion is that, as a general rule, it is decidedly best to train young men... it is found that (their) superior docility renders it much easier to make valuable public servants of them than of those more advanced in life" and furthermore that, "A young man who has not made trial of any other profession will be induced to enter that of the civil service on a much more moderate remuneration than would suffice to attract him in a few years."

There were a number of advantages to Northcote-Trevelyan's plan for recruiting those early in their career and keeping them:

i.   As well as being a high integrity system it was also a competent one, bringing in people on merit. It made a civil service career a respectable one for social advancement.

ii. It produced a professional service where expertise was not discarded with a change of government.

iii. Its permanence provided an antidote to the short term horizons of politicians.

iv. It was respected by all political parties who could rely on it when it was their turn to take over power.

v.   It was largely self sufficient, providing services from within its own resources. This again helped to control the culture.

vi. It minimised transition costs with a change of government.

The system introduced following Northcote-Trevelyan has served well for many years. But, although many of the characteristics described above need to be retained there are problems with the closed system. The assumption of a career for life was previously an asset but can become a liability; a dilemma which will become more acute as the retirement age rises. An excessive sense of hierarchy means people move slowly up the organisation, being promoted when the organisation is ready rather than when they are ready to take on greater responsibility. There are issues of culture: speed of reaction and ability to innovate, a focus on process rather than outcome.

Today we are determined to recruit from as wide a pool of people as possible. Shortly after being appointed Head of the Home Civil Service I referred to "a permanent civil service, not permanent civil servants". Quite apart from the arguments for fairness and equity in recruitment, there are two strong business reasons for this approach. Firstly, it enables us to access more talent, and a greater range of experience and skills. In considering where to draw finance directors from, for instance, it makes a great deal of sense to look to the wider finance officer community than just to the civil service. Similarly, external experience in the wider public, private and voluntary sectors can be valuable.

The impact of these changing patterns of recruitment are evident in the changing profile of the senior civil service. One in five members of the current senior civil service were recruited from outside and one in four board level posts are now filled by people recruited from outside the service. These numbers are likely to increase. We will not reach a stage where all posts are advertised externally, and a strong drive to develop our own talent will remain (as there is in most organisations). A clear majority of civil servants in future will be those who have entered the service relatively young – although hopefully a number of these will seek some experience in other sectors and bring it back with them. This level of continuity is important because of the extent to which the civil service's strength as an organisation comes from its values. Continued cohesion and flexibility as an organisation depends on retaining these, and it will be important that they are not diluted.

The second reason for seeking to bring in and develop a wider range of talent is simply to do the job better. Success in developing public services that reflect the needs of different customers will be limited if civil servants, and the senior civil service in particular, all have the same background. A higher proportion of women, those from ethnic minorities and more disabled people are needed. Real world experience of service delivery in public services is also needed. We are moving in the right direction, but there is still some way to go.

Communications

For the first time, the role of strategic communications and marketing in policy development is being taken seriously. Some people, on hearing these words coupled together, assume that the function being described is persuading people to buy the product you want to sell them. This is absolutely not the role being described. A strategic communications and marketing role begins by developing a better understanding of what customers want, and feeds this back in to the development of the product – in this case policy. Departments are starting to build this sort of function - some are further advanced than others – and it is having significant impact on how policies are made.

Conclusion

It would be naïve to suggest that, once all the changes described here are implemented, the civil service will not need to undergo further change for many years more. Past history shows this. Although specific waves of change can be picked out, associated with committee reports or white papers, in fact the service, like any other successful organisation, adapts and evolves continuously. So whilst there are points of continuity with Fulton, the differences with the service of the 60s are substantial. The characteristic of flexibility and ethos described by Fulton remains equally valid today.

"The civil service has to be flexible enough to serve governments of any political complexion – whether they are committed to extend or in certain respects reduce the role of the state. Throughout it has to remember that it exists to serve the whole of society".

But many of the criticisms noted by Fulton – for instance the lack of contact between the service and the rest of the community, the lack of management ability, the lack of consideration given to people's skills and personal preferences as central decisions were taken about postings – have long since been tackled.

As the environment continues to change, so will the civil service. Progress in using technology to deliver better services will continue, and continue to improve, as will management and organisational techniques. In summation, it is not enough for the civil service to look good, or to be seen to be good, we have to do good too.

The set of reforms that I am currently putting in place are developing the capacity of the service so that better outcomes are achieved, both in services delivered directly and in those delivered in partnership. The ability of the service to respond to changes in future is also improving. I am confident, therefore, that the civil service is well placed to adapt to continuing change.

The Economy and the State

Gus O'Donnell argues that the growth in both the role and size of the state means that its own productivity is now crucial to overall national economic performance. The principles of an impartial, professional, permanent civil service remain highly relevant – the challenge is to define professional government and adapt accordingly.

Gus O'Donnell CB

Gus O'Donnell started his working life as academic economist lecturing at the University of Glasgow, having studied at Warwick and Oxford Universities (Nuffield College). He joined the Treasury in 1979, working on project appraisal guidelines, monetary policy, housing, defence and international trade in a sequence of jobs, often working to Nigel Lawson when he was Financial Secretary.

He was appointed First Secretary at the British Embassy in Washington in the mid 1980s learning diplomatic skills and learning about the entrepreneurial talents of Americans. He came back to work briefly as Nigel Lawson's Press Secretary. When John Major took over after Lawson's resignation, he remained as Press Secretary and moved to No10 when John Major became Prime Minister.

After four years in this most intense and exhilarating of jobs he returned to the relatively quiet pastures of the Treasury dealing with monetary policy during the introduction of inflation targeting. He returned to Washington this time as the UK's Executive Director on the boards of the International Monetary Fund and The World Bank. He was recalled after only 18 months to work with the new Labour Government on macroeconomic policy and international finance issues.

He was also made Head of the government Economic Service covering around 800 economists working across government. In July 2002 he was made Permanent Secretary of the Treasury. He is also a member of the Civil Service Management Board and has been closely involved in developing Sir Andrew Turnbull's agenda to develop "a Civil Service that delivers." He recently completed a review of the relationship between the Inland Revenue, Customs and Excise and the Treasury.

The Relationship between Economy and State

"Commerce and manufactures can seldom flourish in any state in which there is not a certain degree of confidence in the justice of government."
Adam Smith, *The Wealth of Nations*, 1776

I: Economy and State: The Northcote-Trevelyan context

The Northcote-Trevelyan reforms of 1854 took place against a background of dramatic change in the UK economy in the preceding half century. The Industrial Revolution had gathered such pace that half the British population lived in urban areas by 1851, the year the nation showed off its unchallenged global economic leadership with the Great Exhibition in the Crystal Palace.

With an upheaval of this magnitude, the economic and social transformation created pressure on state institutions to adapt to the changing nation. Over the course of the nineteenth and early part of the twentieth centuries there was a decisive, though not always obvious or smooth, shift away from the institutions of state acting as a defender and promoter of established, mainly agrarian interests, towards becoming a more neutral player in society, concentrating instead on the promotion of a more broadly defined national interest.

Politically, this change was manifested in the gradual extension of the franchise (though full, universal suffrage was not in place until 1918), the removal of the property qualification for MPs in 1861 and the introduction of the secret ballot in 1872. Politically, the repeal of the Corn Laws in 1846 was a devastating blow to the perception of parliament and government as the defender of exclusively agrarian interests and a landmark victory for the new economy. Sandwiched in the middle of these developments is Northcote-Trevelyan, which transformed the civil service from being another arm of the state governed by patronage and established interests into a professional cadre of impartial administrators dedicated to serving the wider national interest, the core values of which still persist. Cumulatively, these changes made the government at the end of the nineteenth century more alert to broader economic, social and political trends and developments than the public institutions of a century earlier.

Despite all this, the extent of this transformation can be exaggerated. Lloyd George's successful introduction of national insurance and unsuccessful attempt to enact a land tax to finance it, was challenged by senior Treasury officials who sought to undermine the Chancellor's reforms.

"The Government seem to me to be going straight on the rocks financially (and perhaps otherwise), and nobody will listen to me when I tell them so… I cannot believe that your House will swallow the Budget if the mature infant turns out to be anything like the embryo which I now contemplate daily with horror."
Sir George Murray, Permanent Secretary to the Treasury, to former Prime Minister Lord Roseberry, inciting the peer to oppose the Budget of his own Chancellor, 1908.

This extraordinary quote is proof that Sir George Murray, the then Permanent Secretary, was deliberately inciting a sworn political enemy of the Chancellor's to block the Budget, and was doing so in writing on Treasury notepaper.[1] Similarly, tax reforms in the twentieth century met strong Treasury resistance.[2] Events of this sort are worth remembering when reference is made to a bygone age of unimpeachable propriety and professionalism in the civil service. As ever, the reality was rather more complex.

The degree to which the economic environment in which the Northcote-Trevelyan civil service emerged differs from the contemporary one should not be underestimated, nor should the importance of these differences. Two differences are obvious and important – first, the scale of economic activity and secondly, public perceptions of the legitimate role of the state.

First, on the scale of economic activity, although the United Kingdom in 1851 was an economic superpower, with undisputed technological and trading pre-eminence, it was not the world's largest economy in terms of Gross Domestic Product. The four largest economies were China, India, the UK and the United States in that order, reflecting the sheer size of the populations of the two Asian countries. In the contemporary world however, advances in productivity, fuelled by technology, have fundamentally altered the world economic order.[3] The UK, with just 60 million people, now has a substantially bigger economy than both China, with 1.2 billion people, and India, with just over one billion.

In the nineteenth century the techniques of industrialisation were applied to international transport and communications. International trade increased and new global product, labour and capital markets were forged. These changes transformed the economic capacity of the global economy. In product markets, trading patterns were transformed by the use of steam power for ocean-going ships. The level of world trade (defined by the ratio of world exports to GDP) increased from 2 per cent in 1800 to 10 per cent in 1870 and 21 per cent in 1913. Labour forces became increasingly urbanised, with agriculture's share of employment falling from 40 per cent of the UK workforce in 1820 to just 16 per cent in 1890. Financial markets became increasingly sophisticated as a result of revolutionary changes in communications. This combination of factors helped to create an increasingly global economy on a completely different scale to preceding centuries.

How did this economic revolution affect what was seen as the legitimate role of the state? The Industrial Revolution brought pressure on the institutions of state to move away from a role of protector of traditional interests. Many of the champions of change, notably Peel and Gladstone, subscribed to the emerging consensus among the dominant theorists and practitioners of political economy about the limited role of the state. Gladstone's dictum was that money was best left to "fructify in the pockets of the people". He instructed officials to write on both sides of paper for efficiency. Trevelyan's role in framing the policy response to the Irish Famine of the mid to late 1840s was also controversial. All these examples demonstrate that the framers of the mid-Victorian civil service envisaged a government restricted to national defence and diplomacy, colonial administration, basic law and order and extremely limited social intervention.[4]

However, emerging social pressures, particularly in the second half of the nineteenth century, led to gradual rudimentary state involvement in social affairs. The Disraeli administration (1874–1880) was particularly active. State intervention gradually emerged in areas like the workplace (notably factories, mines and ships), and in embryonic form in education and transport. State involvement in law and order was significantly enhanced with the establishment of a national prison service in 1877. However, as late as 1890 there were just 50,000 civil servants, an increase from the pre-Northcote-Trevelyan figure of 32,000. State administration as a percentage of Gross Domestic Product was just below 10 per cent. So the activities of government at the end of the nineteenth century would have been easily recognisable to Northcote and Trevelyan.

Half a century later things had radically changed. Social pressures, and in particular two prolonged wars of national survival and the Great Depression, transformed the state into a much larger economic player, becoming a purchaser and often a provider of public services and social insurance. The intellectual basis was Keynesian economics. Following a period of dramatic expansion after 1945 the debate has, particularly since the late 1970s, focused once again on the appropriate role of government. The public sector has withdrawn from many activities, most obviously from running a range of commercial businesses. But the terms of the debate have shifted dramatically from the Northcote-Trevelyan context; staffing in the civil service rose to over 400,000 before the Second World War, and by 1970 had crossed the half a million mark, around the same figure as today.

In the early Northcote-Trevelyan era reform was undoubtedly needed to end cronyism and nepotism, and to create meritocracy. The fundamental skill set for this new administrative cadre however revolved around the policy advice and *consigliore* function. What would nowadays be called 'delivery' skills were confined largely to the military and colonial services.

II: Economy and state: the 21st century context

Fast forward to 2005: the UK remains a substantial economic power, the fourth largest in the world, but some way behind the leader, the United States, in both size and productivity. Globally, excepting traumatic interruptions such as the two world wars and the Great Depression, economies have continued to hurtle relentlessly towards global competition in global markets.

The pace of change in communications continues to accelerate, as does technological advance in information technology. Computing speed and storage capacity have progressed at an exponential rate over the last three decades; between 1970 and 1999, the cost of 1 megahertz of processing power fell from $7,601 to 17 cents. There is now an academic and political consensus that continuing globalisation, and in particular the emergence of China and India as potential economic superpowers, significantly alters the strategic context for the UK economy.[5] The UK economy, rather than seeking to compete in the same markets, needs to focus on high value added business, where skills, productivity and flexibility are at a premium.

It is now accepted that the state has a significant role in the economic and social infrastructure of advanced economies, most obviously in areas like education, skills and transport, but also indirectly through what one might call the 'soft' economic infrastructure of any nation, a wide range of issues including, for example, national security, law and order, and public health.

The issues arising from this are manifold. At the most basic level, the fact that the state is responsible for around two fifths of economic activity means that its own productivity is critical to the overall national economic performance.[6] The output of public services must also be properly measured, and Sir Tony Atkinson's recent report is an important step forward in tackling this issue.[7] Moreover, the state is a much more active player in the modern era than in mid-

Victorian times in terms of the incentives structures around employment, savings and so on through the tax and benefit system.

Most fundamentally for the civil service, the contemporary debate is not so much about whether or not the state should be involved in key services like health, education, transport, but what is the most effective method of delivery. In health, education and crime, no major political party has sought to move away from the state acting as a guarantor that services will be provided, but there has been much debate about public versus private, central versus local, the role of targets, and so on. The centre – Whitehall – has had to become much more aware of the range of stakeholders on whom it relies to deliver services, including the wider public sector, local government, the voluntary sector, and private firms.

III: What this means for the 21st century civil service

The principles and vision articulated by Northcote and Trevelyan – an impartial, professional, permanent civil service – remain highly relevant and the key word is professional. But as a result of dramatic change in the economic and social structures since Northcote-Trevelyan, the professional skills required have changed profoundly. To survive and flourish, the challenge for the civil service of the future is to define professional government and adapt accordingly.

This could be a précis of the Fulton report of 1968, with its attack on the amateur official culture and marginalisation of professional skills in the civil service. Sir John Bourn, now head of the National Audit Office, who was seconded to the Fulton inquiry earlier in his career, has commented that Fulton represented a move to a third phase in civil service history post Northcote-Trevelyan.[8] In the first phase, up to the first world war, administration focused on compliance with rules, and indeed many of the formal processes of parliamentary accountability date from this period. The Treasury, for example, focused far more on its finance ministry role than its economics functions, and took a fairly legalistic view of its financial responsibilities.[9] This reflected in part the consensus alluded to earlier about the strict limitations on government activity. The second period, from after the First World War until Fulton, saw the emergence of the civil service as the dominant policy making institution in the country as the state struggled to meet the awesome challenges of two world wars and economic crisis in the inter-war period. Fulton signified that emphasis on policy was no longer enough; what mattered was results, and the civil service could expect to be scrutinised for what it delivered.

Considerable changes for the better have been made already in the civil service in the latter part of the twentieth century. The quality of management is one obvious example – gone are the days when a Permanent Secretary, en route to giving evidence to Fulton, asked his private secretary: "What is a line manager, and am I one?"[10] There have been dramatic institutional changes since Fulton, for example next steps agencies as delivery agents at arms length from departments, and significant cultural changes as well, such as greater emphasis on management and career development.

The background to Fulton was the state becoming a large scale provider of services following the creation of the welfare state in 1945. In the decades since Fulton, public expectations about how the state should function, and in particular how services should be provided, have changed significantly, as highlighted starkly in the American context in Elaine Kamarck's essay elsewhere in this book. I will highlight five key challenges in the conclusion.

Firstly, even greater sophistication is needed in the traditional policy and analytical function of the civil service. Politicians and administrators have long grappled with the impact of their decisions on the economy and on individual behaviour; indeed it was a feature of Trevelyan's own tenure at the Treasury. In the modern era, the role of the economic policy adviser, as in previous decades, is to analyse the impact of tax and benefits on individual economic choices and behaviour, such as decisions to save or invest. But today's analyst could also be faced with subjects like public health (through the debate on tobacco taxes for example) and the environment (with the climate change levy). It is vital that the impact of policy on incentives and behaviour is properly understood.

Secondly, continuing to transform the civil service as an agent of delivery when consumer expectations are higher than ever. This is not just about improving the capacity of government departments as managers and providers. Many key public services are provided through other agents, involving one or more players from the wider public sector or the private or voluntary sectors. So the more fundamental challenge is to foster an ability within the civil service to work through others.

The third challenge is the demand for greater accountability and transparency, reflecting both the importance of services provided by government and the increase in information flows in the 21st century. The civil service has an historic, if sometimes unfair, reputation for secrecy. This culture is unsustainable when information about the performance of many public services is easily and immediately accessible on the Internet. Freedom of information legislation also marks a change in the relationship between citizen and state. The increase in media outlets and penetration increases the demand for information about public services.

Fourthly, to deal with these challenges a greater specialisation within the civil service is undoubtedly needed along with the deployment of professional expertise including finance, information technology, human resources and communications. Sir Peter Gershon's report of July 2004 on the public sector focused on efficiency. In the wider political debate on savings and staff reductions the critical recommendations on improving financial management in government and the emphasis on cleverer use of IT are often missed.[11]

Finally, and linked to the point about specialisms, is that the civil service, like the private sector, needs to have a flexible labour market which can adjust to the demands of the age, continues to increase skill levels and is adroit in its recruitment and retention policies.

Contemporary civil service leaders have to face up to these five challenges in order to shape the service of the future. They are daunting hurdles and it is tempting to see them as insurmountable. David Walker, writing in *The*

Guardian, likened the modern Permanent Secretary to "an administrative black belt, able to read a balance sheet while giving sensitive attention to personnel while offering ministers acute and politically nuanced advice on highly complicated questions".

Modern senior civil servants have to take an interest in a much broader range of issues than some of their predecessors and step outside the comfort zone of policy advice. But perhaps a better approach is to accept that no single individual is likely to master the range of issues – policy and delivery; specialist and generic – and that therefore the focus for civil service leaders should be on building a strong and balanced team with the range of skills to deliver high quality outcomes in a complex world to a public with high expectations. As the Cabinet Office noted, "the role of the Permanent Secretary has become bigger and tougher, and human beings do not come in the shape that is needed to meet single-handedly all the challenges of this new tougher role…[So] the focus should be on the top team, not the top job. The Permanent Secretary should focus on the leader role, because that cannot be delegated to anyone else".

A strong and balanced top team will require a diverse range of skills and experience. In this context the Northcote-Trevelyan concept of recruitment through fair and open competition is worth re-considering.

Given the changes in the composition of British society, in particular vastly increased social mobility, the increasing participation of women in the workforce and far greater ethnic diversity in the UK population, the civil service should strive to reflect the population it serves.

But diversity is also about the range of experience and expertise. This is not just about bringing in outside talent into the civil service, and ensuring proper professional training for career civil servants, important though both these are. The concept of the 'lifer', the official who enters a department after university and stays in the same place until retirement, has to be challenged. In a recent staff survey, half the Treasury's senior civil service said they were considering seeking a post outside the department in the next five years. This is a positive indication of active career management by staff, not a threat to the organisation.

In short, in future the civil service has to cast the net wider in order to get the best people bringing the best blend of skills. The civil service should be gaining from the experiences of a cross-section of society. So there should be no conflict between the principle of merit and diversity; indeed a more diverse civil service is an essential ingredient in improving performance.

The Professional Skills for Government Agenda, launched by the Cabinet Secretary, Sir Andrew Turnbull in October 2004, marks a useful contribution to meeting the challenge, not least by its explicit recognition of operational and corporate services specialisms in the civil service and the plans for continuous professional development in each part of them.

To conclude, the Northcote-Trevelyan template for the civil service is necessary for a high performing civil service. The civil service will not survive if it loses the greatest bequest of Northcote-Trevelyan: a reputation for impartiality and meritocracy. But whilst the values of Northcote-Trevelyan are a *necessary* condition for the civil service of the future, they are not *sufficient*. What is needed in addition is an ongoing, rigorous analysis of what the professional challenges for government are in the years ahead, an honest assessment of how well – or badly – we are equipped to deal with them, and the flexibility, determination and leadership to bring about the required change.

Notes

1. The author is indebted to Professor Iain McLean of Nuffield College, Oxford, for bringing this correspondence to his attention. Elsewhere in the collection of letters from Murray to Roseberry, to whom the former had served as private secretary during the latter's tenure as Prime Minister, the Permanent Secretary is openly scathing about Lloyd George and his colleagues. In one letter, he lets it be known that he believes the administration to be "incomparably the worst Government that we have had since the Reform Bill". In another, he refers to Lloyd George as "my Welsh goat, who feeds happily enough out of my hand at present". The papers are held by the National Library of Scotland.

2. For a fuller account, see *Just Taxes: The politics of taxation in Britain 1914-1979* Martin Daunton, Cambridge University Press, 2002

3. *The World Economy: A Millennial Perspective* Angus Maddison, OECD 2001

4. For an interesting modern account of the philosophy of the 'minimalist' state, see Robert Nozick's *Anarchy, State and Utopia* (Acumen, 1977). For a very different view, see John Rawls, *A Theory of Justice* (Harvard 1971)

5. See for example Martin Wolf's *Why Globalization Works*, Yale University Press 2004. The issues and some of the relevant literature are also discussed in *Long term global economic challenges and opportunities for the UK*, HM Treasury, December 2004

6. For a discussion of this and wider issues around public service productivity, see *Public Services: Meeting the Productivity Challenge* HM Treasury, April 2003

7. *Atkinson Review Final Report: Measurement of Government and Productivity for the National Accounts*, Palgrave, January 2005

8. Lecture by Sir John Bourn to the Chartered Institute of Public Finance and Accounting, 1998.

9. See for example the paper written by R.E. Welby, Permanent Secretary from 1885–1894, on the organisation of the Treasury, which deals almost exclusively with the formal procedures for financing and debt management, with almost no evidence of economic policymaking capacity. This memorandum is printed in Lord Bridges' *The Treasury*, George, Allen & Unwin 1964

10. See Peter Hennessy, *Whitehall*, Pimlico (latest edition 2001)

11. *Releasing resources to the front line: report by Sir Peter Gershon*, Cabinet Office, July 2004

CHANGING **TIMES**

Social Issues and Government

Gerard Lemos argues that advances in science and technology mean there is a continuing need for innovation in the social domain to tackle 'the problems that won't go away'. As the only ones with an incentive to make a positive difference, government and the voluntary sector must be persistent and expert in social innovation, even when irreversible success is elusive.

Gerard Lemos CMG

Gerard Lemos is the author of numerous reports and books on social policy including *The Communities We Have Lost and Can Regain* (with Michael Young), *The Search for Tolerance: Challenging and changing racist attitudes and behaviour among young people* and *Military History: Homelessness amongst ex-service people*.

He has advised a range of UK Government departments on social policy and taught at universities in Britain and in many other countries. Gerard Lemos is a Civil Service Commissioner, Chairman of Notting Hill Housing Group and Deputy Chair of the British Council. He is also the Chairman of the Banking Code Standards Board, a regulator of the retailing banking industry and Chair of the board of the Akram Khan Dance Company. In 2001 he received a CMG for services to the British Council.

Beyond Reach: Government, the Civil Service and the Wicked Issues

Elsewhere in this collection others have written of the need for government and the civil service to enhance emerging capabilities and developing new ones. Making policy and standing back whilst others deliver in local government, the NHS, or the Armed Forces is no longer regarded as an adequate or acceptable stance for the civil service. That would now be characterised as smug, otherworldly and perhaps even arrogant. Civil servants now know they must engage closer to the front line of the delivery of public services. They must, as it were, become more retail and less wholesale in their relationships with citizens and those who provide citizens with public services. In order to do that effectively, they need to gain experience of successful delivery in government and elsewhere as they rise through the ranks. They also need the support of professional structures in departments that must change to resemble more closely private and public sector organisations operating face to face with consumers. Hence civil service departments are enhancing financial and human resources management, IT, communication and marketing skills and so on. Many of these changes are no longer just on the drawing board; they have become part of the emerging reality of civil service life. Policy is still a core competence of the civil service, but no longer the only one. Perhaps it never was the only one, but enhancing other capabilities has come to feel more urgent in recent years. But will these changes be enough?

An equation often quoted in management and leadership development circles is germane here: The rate of internal change within an organisation has to be at least equal to, or greater than, the rate of external change. The changes that are happening within the government and the civil service may not be fast enough or far enough advanced. We are, most agree, living through an era of accelerated technological and scientific change. The risk of disappointment or even failure lies, to a degree, in not keeping pace. These changes are now well documented and part of public discourse and frequently referred to by other contributors to this collection. Less thoroughly debated, understood or resolved upon are the consequential and unpredictable forces of social change, some of them seismic, unleashed by these mostly benign advances in science and technology.

Above the waterline, globalisation in many of its manifestations brings changes in, most notably, the manner and matter of international trade, national and international labour markets and global migration. We are no longer a world just of exchanges. We have become a world of flows: flows of goods, services, information, ideas, knowledge, trends and, of course, flows of people. And the impact is to be seen as much in the domestic, private space, which is also being transformed, as it is evident in the economic, political and public space. I will seek to isolate a few trends of relevance to the future practice of government and, in particular, the civil service, though there are undoubtedly others:

- The demography of our contemporary society has no antecedents. Never before have there been so many old people and so few young people. This perhaps partly explains why the vastly depleted number of young people are so readily characterised as a problem by the vastly increased number of older people.

- The social and economic role of women has been transformed, even though gender equality remains elusive. The understanding of men as social and economic actors struggles to catch up and keep pace with a transformed labour market populated more than ever before by women with assertive ideas of themselves and their futures.

- Childhood is being re-defined. No longer the age of innocence, childhood is coming to be seen as an era to be almost entirely given over to the acquisition of skills and qualities in preparation for later post-industrial employment. Childhood as a traumatic time for some has also come to be more widely recognised, though the experiences are not new.

- Global migration is bringing together in British cities groups of migrants with no shared heritage of empire, commonwealth, religion, culture or language. The new diversity is post-post colonial. Immigrants are no longer large groups of people from a small number of former colonies. Instead they are small groups of people from a large number of (often very troubled) places all over the world. Amidst this new diversity, if division is to be avoided, our common citizenship needs greater explicit articulation. Implicit shared understandings and acceptances no longer suffice.

All this gives rise to policy challenges, many new, some rather more longstanding. These can loosely be collected under the following headings:

- Scientific changes without a backdrop of a settled social or ethical consensus
- The 'dark shadows' of globalisation
- The downsides of prosperity
- The consequences of longevity
- The shifting tectonics of gender and family relations
- The problems that just won't go away

Scientific and technological innovation can fall out of alignment with the social and ethical consensus. That is the first set of issues that seems sometimes beyond the reach of current policymaking mechanisms and processes: food safety and genetic crop modification, human embryo research and stem cell technology, animal cloning and climate change to name a few of the most hotly debated. The regulatory and transparency arrangements for biotechnology in the UK are as good as anywhere in the world, but the feeling lingers that things are moving faster than policy and practice. The best policies are based on evidence, but in areas of emerging technology, conclusive evidence on which to base definitive policy is not yet available; nor will it be for decades, perhaps generations. But, as far as incipient problems are concerned, absence of evidence of a problem should not be seen as evidence of absence of that problem. Notwithstanding well-meant and honestly felt reassurances from politicians and civil servants, there may still be a problem. Until firm evidence is provided of the safety of genetically modified food, for example, the opening position behind a veil of ignorance is understandably scepticism. Trust in institutional pronouncements is put at a premium.

The second set of issues that still feel beyond reach are those that emerge as a darker collateral to the processes of globalisation themselves: the international drugs trade, human trafficking or the illegal international trade in arms. The French philosopher Baudrillard observed, quizzically, about the relations between the North and the South that the developed world has sent weapons and debt to the developing world and they have returned payment in drugs. A crass over-simplification of course, but a disturbing thought nevertheless. These shadow consequences of globalisation are entwined with the increasing and increasingly pressing concern with global security and terrorism. Groups like Al Qaeda or the drug cartels of Colombia are not susceptible to the elegantly dressed range of sticks threatened and carrots offered by conventional diplomacy. These groups are not organisations in any conventionally understood sense. They have structures, but they do not have a single leader or a clear chain of command. They are not based in buildings and they communicate using the very latest technologies. They are evanescent networks operating behind a globally recognised 'brand' which has a beguiling but profoundly misleading sense of familiarity. Osama bin Laden is not like Saladin at the head of a well-organised anti-western army. He is, as far as anyone can tell, at the centre of a web of constantly shifting alliances, interests and configurations.

Prosperity has brought forth intractable dilemmas of policy and values. Environmental degradation is already far advanced and the pace of further degradation is growing as industrialisation and prosperity spread across countries such as India and China, which have not hitherto used non-renewable resources at the same rate as the West. That gap is now closing. Fast developing countries take the understandable view that they should not be constrained from using resources and emitting wasteful and harmful by-products by international treaties promoted by countries which industrialised without the constraints they now seek to impose on others. Even the most optimistic forecasts only prognosticate a slowdown in the rate of environmental degradation. No one dares to suggest it can be reversed.

Prosperity has also contributed to longevity and changes in the structure of family life. Longevity, whilst a huge social advance, has brought forth the indignities of the new pandemics of extreme old age, particularly Alzheimer's disease. The third age may have become, pensions permitting, an age of freedom from responsibility. The fourth age of those who are infirm and without work, health or wealth, on the other hand, is troubling, costly and existentially alienating both for very old people themselves as well as for their relatives.

The twentieth century also saw fundamental and wider shifts in social attitudes to the roles, rights and responsibilities of women and children. Eric Hobsbawm, one of the great historians of the twentieth century, observed crisply in his study of that era, "Women work because children don't." As a result of these tectonic attitudinal shifts, problems such as domestic violence or child sexual abuse, previously contained in a private, patriarchal realm, are now exposed to harsh public censure and the subject of urgent calls for government action. Those opaque power structures of family life as was now seem anachronistic at best; at worst they are brutal, oppressive and traumatising.

Lastly, there are a set of issues that simply won't go away and not for want of trying or for lack of expenditure on the part of government, charities and lots of others: homelessness, the problems of drug users, mental health, repeat criminal offending, teenage pregnancies, racial hatred and intolerance – again this is not an exhaustive list of what have come to be known as the 'wicked issues'.

Although all the issues are described in this essay as being currently beyond reach, the civil service, prompted by government policy from all parties in power, have responded and often with some effectiveness. Things do get better, much better, but no one would seriously argue that all the solutions have been found and their successful application is only a matter of time and money. Financial and other resources have been made available. Much else has also been done: the evidence base is often clearly established, partnerships have been promoted, regulators and inspectors have been given the power to challenge, compare, remonstrate and correct and there has been no shortage of publicity and exhortation. But irreversible success remains elusive on many subjects. Evidently there is a continuing need for innovation in the social as well as technological domain and government and the voluntary sector are the only ones with any moral or other incentives to make a positive difference.

Some indications of the areas where innovation is needed are starting to emerge. New products and services are certainly needed in the public domain. But new ways of delivering them are also urgently sought: new structures, new organisational forms, engaging sectors other than the public sector in the delivery of public services and, crucially, new ways of garnering reliable information and disseminating it to the citizenry. The internet remains potentially a far more valuable tool to the public sector than the commercial world. Its capacity for creating well-informed consumers of, for example, medical services is already well established. The empowerment effect is untold and the lie is given to the idea that people no longer trust each other. Trust in institutions, as opposed to trust in people, is what is in question. Furthermore, as Onora O'Neill has observed in her Reith lectures, transparency and disclosure measures may make organisations more trustworthy while simultaneously and paradoxically breeding mistrust amongst the citizenry in those self same institutions. As R W Johnson waspishly observed about public institutions, "It's not the state we're in that's the problem, it's the state they're in."

There are other straws in the wind about new structures and systems of delivery: large corporations have now learnt the value-added to be gained from network and team working. Command and control hierarchies are seen as expensive, out of date and likely to crush the creative spirit of those they seek to influence and harness. In the public and voluntary sectors more thinking is needed about how government through the civil service can invest in networks of innovation and delivery, while continuing to meet the higher duties of public audit and accountability. The now manifold public sector partnerships could not always be accurately described as networks of innovation. On the contrary, they are seen as opportunistic, evanescent, often conflictual and sometimes more focused on talking than action.

The final point of relevance to the civil service relates to timescale. Almost none of the problems adumbrated above are susceptible to 'quick wins' (a phrase now too commonly used in government circles). They all require persistent, often small scale innovation, the next innovation building on the last, the re-thinking of old paradigms in every detail, the painstaking accumulation of knowledge and expertise, the making of new chains and fretworks across civil society, the public sector and business and, above all, the fervent hope that the lessons learnt will be learnt faster than the problem will mutate. Promoting social innovation is less like a starburst and more like making a map of the Milky Way.

Political parties and elected governments can create and change the mood music within a society. Values and priorities matter as well as evidence. Capturing the public mood and responding to it, leading when necessary, is one of the highest duties of politicians and political parties. Failure stalks parties and governments that don't read the runes right. But, given the long timescales involved and the intractable nature of many of the problems described, it is the permanent civil service, working with and through others, not just 'here today, gone tomorrow' politicians, that must change to become the archivist of professional memory, the record-keeper of change, the notator and evaluator of innovation and the begetter of networks and new structures and systems. Above all, the permanent civil service must be the impartial, objective and far-sighted adviser on the financial and other investments needed for a better future.

CHANGING **TIMES**

Public Services in a Market Society

Sir Alan Langlands uses the NHS as a case study to demonstrate that the progress of public service depends largely on the *context* – political economy and personalities, the *content* – the substance of what the organisation does, and the *process* – the way in which it does it and tackles change. Public and political aspirations for the NHS remain high and the relationship between the government, the public and the market is delicately poised.

Sir Alan Langlands FRSE

Alan Langlands is the Principal and Vice Chancellor of the University of Dundee. The University is a world ranking research institute and provides a broad range of undergraduate and postgraduate teaching programmes. He also chairs UK Biobank Ltd, a joint venture between the Wellcome Trust and the Medical Research Council.

Alan was the Chief Executive of the National Health Service in England from 1994–2000 where, as the Secretary of State's principal policy adviser for the NHS, he was accountable to Parliament for the effective stewardship of a £42bn revenue budget. He has an international reputation in the development of healthcare policy and as a strategic manager of health services and has advised in many countries including Russia, the USA, Canada and China. He received a Knighthood in the Queen's Birthday Honours list (1998) for his services to the NHS and is a Fellow of the Royal Society of Edinburgh.

Alan is a science graduate of the University of Glasgow and was conferred Doctor of the University in October 2001. He is an Honorary Professor at the University of Warwick Business School. He has been awarded Honorary Fellowships by the Royal College of Physicians, the Royal College of General Practitioners, the Royal College of Surgeons of Edinburgh, the Royal College of Physicians and Surgeons (Glasgow), the Faculty of Public Health Medicine and the Institute of Actuaries.

NHS Specs to Harry Potter

The millennium exhibition at the National Portrait Gallery included a famous black and white photograph. Published by Magee Haywood in 1951 for a Picture Post story about The Princess Theatre in Glasgow it has the title 'Warm and Happy' but is often referred to simply as 'NHS Specs'. It shows a small, bespectacled boy (probably aged about eight) wrapped up in a coat and scarf in front of the Princess Theatre in Glasgow. The boy was anonymous but I always think of him as Freddie Graham.

Freddie is now easing towards sixty-two and, pensions permitting, the possibility of early retirement. He is a product of the post-war welfare state. Free specs, free dental care and his tonsils removed by an eminent ENT surgeon 'just as a precaution'. As a child his family holidays were in the seaside towns of the Clyde, reached by a paddle steamer which sailed from industrial Glasgow passing the shipyards of Govan, Port Glasgow and Greenock.

Freddie has done well for himself. He learned to swim at the public baths, borrowed books from the public library, went to good schools and was supported by generous grants through university before following a successful career in banking and financial services. He bought his own house in the late 1960s and, courtesy of Margaret Thatcher, he also bought his parents their council house in the 1980s.

With two children and one grandchild called Jennifer, Freddie now swims at his exclusive leisure club, he buys books on-line from Amazon and he holidays in Madeira in the spring and New England in the fall (he prefers this term to autumn). As he drives to the airport in Glasgow, he notices the growing concentration of digital media companies at Atlantic Quay and the old light bulb factory which has been converted into some very smart art deco apartments (he prefers this term to flats).

Despite these pretensions, Freddie has not forgotten his roots. He realises that many of his generation got trapped in the council estates of Glasgow and is conscious of the city's poor health record and the problems of teenage pregnancy and drug abuse. Despite the many other changes in his life, he believes in the NHS and the principle of a comprehensive system of health care based on need and free at the point of delivery. On a bad day he gets frustrated by the inefficiency of the NHS and the fact that 'unlike the financial services industry, it has failed to change with the times.'

Freddie had almost forgotten about his NHS specs – his last pair of vari-focals cost in excess of £300 but he did get a free pair of prescription sunglasses, very handy as he drives in an easterly direction to the office every morning and pretty stylish in the cobbled streets of Funchal on Madeira. So there he was reading aloud from *Harry Potter and the Philosopher's Stone* to amuse Jennifer. It was Dudley Dursley's birthday party at number four, Privet Drive when we got our first real description of Harry, Dudley's favourite punch bag – 'Harry had a thin face, knobbly knees, black hair and bright green eyes. He wore round glasses held together with a lot of Sellotape because of all the times Dudley had punched him on the nose…'

Freddie looked out that old photograph of him standing outside the Princess Theatre wearing his NHS specs but Jennifer was unimpressed. But soon Harry, wearing the same specs, was a multi-million pound marketing phenomenon – beaming from multiplex cinemas, the window displays at Waterstones and the covers of CDs, DVDs, computer games and even Jennifer's bed linen. Freddie has a good track record of handling the lifelong process of maintaining continuity and accommodating change but these specs provided a real test – how should public services be developing in a market society? And how would the Hogwarts express have coped with rail privatisation?

The evolution of public services

The first question which here presents itself is, whether it is better to train young men for the discharge of the duties which they will afterwards have to perform, or to take men of mature age, who have previously acquired experience in other walks of life?

Northcote and Trevelyan 1854

In his masterpiece on Whitehall, Peter Hennessy describes this passage of analysis as the pumping heart of the 'new blood' arguments put forward about senior civil service appointments in the 1980s and early 90s. As a result of this argument I was appointed (from the NHS) to the post of NHS Chief Executive, based in the Department of Health.

My NHS roots explain my tendency to think of public service mainly in terms of delivering positive outcomes for the people who use services. It also explains why health care is the main example for exploring the theme of public services in a market society in this essay, although I nevertheless respect the mainstream of the civil service with its *independence, character, ability and experience to be able to advise, assist, and to some extent, influence those who are from time to time set over them.*

The definition of public services is becoming elusive but it should embrace all organisations and partnerships that work for the public, using public money. Most of these are public sector organisations whose services are used directly by members of the public or who are responsible for less visible activities, such as regulation and policy development. But the use of public money to provide public services is no longer limited to the public sector and this poses new challenges for accountability.

True understanding of the development of public services in a market society also needs an historical perspective and of course a great deal has been written on this subject by Peter Hennessy and many others. Nicholas Timmins' biography of the welfare state is a *tour de force*. It starts with the Beveridge report and his crusade to slay the five giants of want, ignorance, disease, squalor and idleness and traces the ups and downs of British welfare policy from the early 1940s with a focus on housing, education, social security, the NHS and employment. An extended definition of public services might have included policing and the criminal justice system. Timmins follows Beveridge's vision and the development of public services through *the expansion of the 1950s and 1960s, the doubts of the 1970s, the rhetorical, financial and organisational assaults of the 1980s and the mid-life crisis of the 1990s.*

These assaults of the 1980s and early 90s included the introduction of quasi-markets in the British public sector. Julian Le Grand's and Carol Propper's work on the role of central government in a quasi-market in relation to planning and promoting competition is worth re-visiting in the context of supply-side reforms since the late 1990s. Their sense of needing to shift the balance of power from central politicians to local managers also still has resonance. Ewan Ferlie et al took a wider sweep at the new public management in action and developed key insights on restructuring, transformational change, board involvement and the shifting balance of power between managers and the professions. Their work is also worth re-visiting as the early 21st century market reforms take hold.

Timmins seemed to know intuitively that examining the progress of public services demands an understanding of what Andrew Pettigrew calls the *subtle interplay between the context* – the political economy and personalities of the time; *content* – the substance of what the organisation does or the products or services it provides; and *process* – how public service organisations set about their business and tackle issues of development and change. He also has a canny knack of homing in on outcome measures. Critically he makes the point that the welfare state means different things to different people. Over half a century it has affected Freddie Graham's parents, Freddie himself and Freddie's children in many different ways. So what lies in store for Jennifer?

The case of the NHS

The NHS has been a top priority for the present government since 1997. As it moves towards its sixtieth birthday in 2008, it remains a focus of public debate, policy intervention and structural change and, following long periods of low growth, it is now benefiting from higher levels of investment. This is not an attempt at a comprehensive review of NHS policy but I remain positive about the overall direction of travel and I cannot resist just one policy excursion.

Securing our Future Health: Taking a Long Term View prepared by Derek Wanless is the first published attempt to quantify 'the financial and other resources required to ensure that the NHS can provide a publicly funded, comprehensive, high quality service available on the basis of clinical needs and not ability to pay'. This is the most significant policy document of recent times firstly because it is surprising that the government asked the question in this form and secondly because the Wanless Report provides a public baseline for all future spending negotiations affecting the NHS. Wanless traces the main influences on the resourcing of the NHS and social care and his findings have resulted in the promise of further sustained increases in real terms spending until at least 2008.

The Wanless Report also gives new momentum to ensuring that information and communications technology is developed more quickly in support of patient care, that issues of workforce development and skill mix are examined in greater detail and that further steps are taken to streamline the management of the NHS. The strategy of increasing spending whilst striving to use existing resources more efficiently provides the best way forward for a 'publicly funded, comprehensive, high quality service'.

However, yet again this complex management task is being played out against the shifting sands of structural change, a proliferation of new regulatory bodies and a lingering sense of command and control from central government. Once again the emphasis seems to be on the anatomy of the NHS rather that the physiology of health care which critically includes incentives and the motivation of staff. The Wanless prescription of more holistic decision making 'recognising the inter-relationships between many of the resources in the system' is difficult to deliver when people are constantly changing places. Continuity at a time of change is often a good formula.

Enduring challenges

For more than fifty years, the real strength of the NHS has been clarity and constancy of purpose. The fundamental purpose has wide public acceptance and has been restated in legislation by successive governments. In essence it is to secure through the resources available the greatest possible improvement in the physical and mental health of people by:

- promoting health
- preventing ill health
- diagnosing and treating injury and disease, and
- caring for those with long term illness and disability who need the services of the NHS.

The aim is still to provide services on the basis of equal access for equal need, not the ability to pay. However, like every other health system in the world, the NHS is under pressure. Change is endemic in all dimensions and at every level of the service and six key challenges remain.

1. The swing from the collective to the individual

Some analysts such as Uwe Reinhardt believe that the erosion of collective values in society will occur to such a degree that all health systems might eventually have the same three-tier structure: a top tier of fee-for-service medicine for the very rich; a middle tier of insurance-based managed care covering the middle classes; and a third tier of publicly funded 'rough and ready' care for the poor. Government policy is to avoid this route, but expectations are high. Surveys consistently show that the public want more public money to be spent on the NHS, regardless of the overall level of funding. Freddie Graham is not alone in his views that the service has to change with the times and he realises that this will cost money.

The government is committed to improving the NHS and substantial additional money is being invested. However we are all wealthier. People want faster access and more one to one attention. The challenge of sustaining the best of the NHS model should not be underestimated. The government faces a major dilemma as pay inflation and continuing workforce shortages have limited the extra output achieved from increased investment. Supply side reform is central but could the government be forced to adopt an even more radical course, perhaps based on extending current market thinking to include demand side competition? Will NHS dentistry finally go the way of NHS specs and long term care for the elderly and require payment? Will there be more means testing for NHS services?

2. Harnessing innovation in science and technology

Advances in biomedical research are resulting in new forms of diagnosis and treatment: gene mapping and gene therapy, ultrasound treatment of tumours and intravenous treatment at home controlled by a chip. The foresight capacity of the NHS has improved and there are better systems of health technology assessment but the speed of change is breathtaking, making it difficult to keep pace. There is more to come.

The sheer amount of information discovered by the human genome project is staggering but it is only a step towards answering the real question – how do genes work together in a human being? Progress is in two directions – even more sophisticated basic science and more translational research. Large scale population studies will begin to untangle the genetic, environmental and lifestyle determinants of common diseases.

The NHS provides a unique 'test bed' for research and an incentive for the pharmaceutical industry to maintain its presence and a good share of its research funding in this country. NHS Research and Development programmes are well developed and the government is giving priority to promoting the use of research findings as a basis for setting standards and planning services. This needs to continue.

Innovation in information technology and communications also has the potential to revolutionise patient care. The NHS stands to benefit enormously. The national information strategy – Information for Health – made all the key connections, promising:

- lifelong health records which will improve the treatment and care of every person in the country
- the opportunity for faster, seamless care
- a national electronic library of knowledge on best practice for clinicians and on-line information services for patients, and
- the analytical tools that health planners and managers need to make more effective use of resources.

Finally, parallel innovations in private sector industries mean that expectations of what can be delivered in the public sector are rising – convenience and individual tailored services delivered at home are becoming the norm. Once again NHS staff will be expected to respond flexibly to rising public expectations.

3. Changes in the media and increasing political involvement

Digitisation and other advances in the media are resulting in a proliferation of news channels and a growing appetite for human-interest stories. Health care is excellent quarry, particularly when a political angle on news can often be used. The new media also means that the public are seeking out and becoming more familiar with research based information – sometimes in a controlled manner (like NHS Direct) – sometimes not. One recent paper from the US estimated that more than 70,000 websites disseminate health information and more than 50 million people seek health information online. We are only beginning to understand the long term consequences of this in health systems.

Political interest in the NHS is more intense than ever. As media scrutiny increases, the public are increasingly making the link between the performance of domestic public services and the competence of government. The temptation for politicians to get involved in the detail of health care was irresistible from 1997 to 2001 and it remains to be seen whether more recent talk of standing back will be followed through. A serious debate about distancing the NHS from direct political control might well be timely. There must be a way of maintaining proper public accountability whilst liberating the system from overt political interventions and knee-jerk reactions.

Thinking more widely, as the UK is bound closer into political and economic union within Europe, it may be that our national scope to organise, finance and manage the public sector will be constrained by our involvement in the converging European economy. Safe levels of health protection – in relation to medicines, food and measures against communicable diseases – already have to be guaranteed across the Union as a whole and there is growing political, professional and media interest in comparative health systems that is unlikely to go away.

4. The imbalance between demand and supply

Regardless of the actual level of supply and demand in the NHS (which cannot be measured very easily), the perceived difference will grow as expectations rise. The answer cannot just be more of everything. A 2002 British Medical Journal article aimed to show in a comparative study of the NHS and California's Kaiser Permanente that, though the per capita costs of the two systems are broadly the same, there are significant differences in some aspects of performance including access to specialists and waiting times. Although some of the data can be questioned, the article laid out legitimate challenges for the NHS in relation to integration, cost effective care, choice and the use of information technology. The most telling finding of all was that the NHS uses three times as many days of hospital admission per capita as Kaiser. Using increases in the number of acute beds as a measure of improvement is therefore a misjudgement. As Wanless pointed out, people, systems and the interrelationship between the two matter just as much.

There will be a premium on managing these perceptions and an unstoppable requirement to give people the information they need to make choices about their own treatment and care and to influence the development of the services they are funding. Both Labour and the Conservatives focused much of their pre-election rhetoric on the issue of choice. How the influence of individuals can be exercised is one of the big unanswered policy questions. In a speech in 2002, the Secretary of State for Health envisaged an NHS 'where patients can make informed choices about their service and about their care'. He also said that within a few years locally-run primary care will control 75% of the total NHS budget and that professionals and patients will be able to choose from which hospitals – public or private – care is commissioned. This sounds familiar but, as before, it leaves two major tensions unresolved:

- the need to balance, for each individual, the desire to provide care at home or in the community with safe, high quality, cost effective care, and
- the requirement on the Strategic Health Authorities and Primary Care Trusts to assess the needs of the people they serve and to decide (within the resources available to them) how best to meet those needs. This requires an open dialogue with the public and freedom to establish local priorities, both of which have proved difficult to achieve in the past.

5. Changes in the burden of disease

Attention will continue to focus on the impact of ageing and the continuing inequalities in health between rich and poor. There will also be changes in the nature and prevalence of diseases like AIDS, CJD and tuberculosis, increased resistance to antibiotics and threats from changes in the physical environment. Global travel is increasing the risk of transmission of infection and it is not so long ago that the spread of the severe acute respiratory syndrome (SARS) virus was posing a major public health challenge to governments around the world. The long awaited flu pandemic may be brewing and the threat of bioterrorism has also cast a shadow. Risky behaviour particularly amongst the young may also have profound effects in the future. The Chief Medical Officer's strategy for tackling infectious diseases and the development of the Health Protection Agency are therefore important and timely responses. Vigilance is all important.

6. Challenges for the professions

Professional careers in the 21st century are tough and challenging. In most professions the essential elements of a recognisable code of ethics, a system of self regulation and a sense of vocation remain but many aspects of professional life are subject to fundamental change.

There is now a much stronger emphasis on professional accountability shaped by third party regulation, market forces and a tough regime of standards, performance monitoring and mandatory continuing professional development. For many there is also a greater dependence on new technologies, changes at the boundaries between different professions requiring new approaches to teamwork and an overriding imperative to take account of changing public attitudes.

The old approach based on the paternalism of the professions and the blind trust of clients, patients, pupils and customers is consigned to history. The new professionals have to be responsive to the needs and wishes of the people they serve and they have to reflect the broad sweep of modern society and the social, ethnic and economic mix of communities.

Government, universities, professional bodies and employers need to work together to ensure that professionals are prepared and developed to maximise their contribution to the economic, social and cultural development of the country. Bristol, Shipman and Alder Hey knocked the stuffing out of many NHS professionals particularly doctors but public trust and support for the people working in the NHS remains strong and it is time to assimilate the lessons from these difficulties and to move on in a positive way.

Coping with change

The NHS and other health systems across the developed world are facing these six challenges now. So how well is the NHS responding? Progress in the NHS has to be measured against three key results: equity, efficiency and responsiveness.

Equity

Equity can be defined as improving the health of the whole population and reducing variations in health status by targeting resources where needs are greatest. The standardised all cause mortality ratios by social classes for men aged 20–64 in England and Wales are higher among social class 5 than social class 1 – not surprising because the standardised all cause mortality ratios have been reducing in all socio economic classes since the 1970s, but the reduction is lowest in social class 5. There is a similar picture for women. The gap in standardised all cause mortality ratios between social classes grew consistently from the 1970s and whilst this problem has been acknowledged since 1997 the gap remains stubborn and will be slow to close.

The government has pursued a raft of new policies and initiatives to tackle this problem, including Surestart, the work of the social exclusion unit in our worst housing estates and action on smoking and teenage pregnancy.

None of these measures can have an immediate impact on closing the health gap between rich and poor but the Treasury – the driving force behind many of these initiatives – must persist and avoid the temptation to redistribute resources from these areas to shore up NHS provision. Striking the right balance between short term goals and tackling the social determinants of health will be a continuing dilemma for government and NHS leaders.

Efficiency

Efficiency is providing patients with treatment and care that is both effective and good value for money. With the introduction of Primary Care Trusts the NHS is moving towards a national system of 'managed care' – although this is defined as care managed by general practitioners and their teams of nursing and other support staff, not by a third party. A new quality framework is also being embedded to:

- set clear national standards;
- improve the dependability of local delivery systems, and
- ensure that monitoring systems are in place to track progress.

The principle of clinical governance is at the heart of these arrangements. It makes NHS bodies accountable for continuously improving the quality of their services and safeguarding high standards of care by creating an environment which promotes excellence in clinical care. The basic premise underlying these efforts is that people do not fail, but systems allow failure to occur. Clinical governance is about getting the systems and the environment right. It is complemented by the profession's own system of revalidation designed to regularly assess the competence and skills of doctors. Similar approaches are quickly developing for other professional groups and continued effort is required in this area. The new monitoring body – the Healthcare Commission – carries a heavy responsibility. It must avoid a punitive approach and ensure the continued development of good practice.

Responsiveness

I define *responsiveness* simply as meeting the needs and wishes of individual people who use the NHS. This is an area where the government was determined to make its mark but aspirations outstripped the available resources between 1997 and 2001 leaving politicians, the public and the professions feeling frustrated. Nonetheless progress was made (and is now accelerating) on waiting lists and waiting times, investment in buildings and equipment and better access to information. Premature deaths from the major diseases are falling and more treatments are being provided outside hospitals, quickly and to a high standard. By 2010 the NHS budget in the UK is set to grow to more than £70 billion. This whole sum (not just the increases) needs to be mobilised to support positive change with a focus on the quality of services, the cost effectiveness of services and the motivation of staff. In his 1991 Audit Commission lecture, Roy Griffiths cited these three things and said 'I don't believe you can do anything unless you motivate staff'.

A more responsive service depends on the attitudes and skills of staff. It depends on how they are treated. Transforming the NHS is primarily a matter of changing attitudes and behaviour – to be more responsive to patients staff need to motivated, willing to operate in a flexible way. The British public think that the NHS is a poor employer. More enlightened employment practices, more involvement of staff in key decisions and investment in education, training and development are all being used as ways of energising the staff of the NHS. This has been a key area of weakness and will determine the rate of further improvement of the service.

Conclusion

The challenges facing the NHS are being tackled systematically, but public and political aspirations may be difficult to satisfy prompting further pre-emptive changes to the structure and funding of the system. The government's biggest challenge in moving forward is to keep its nerve.

I remain committed to an NHS that after 50 years keeps people healthy and independent and provides them with:

- quick, effective and convenient treatment
- good information about health and health services, and
- high standards of care.
  An NHS that provides:
- a comprehensive system of benefits, as now
- a managed system of primary care
- a new emphasis on clinical accountability, with the professions integrated into management

- effective partnership working, and
- support for local innovation and the rapid replication of good ideas.

We should not be asked to choose just yet between a government-led or a market-led health system. The government through NHS management still has a role to play in promoting equity, efficiency and responsiveness, maintaining checks and balances, planning and capacity building. In time private sector providers will inevitably take more and more responsibility for services but both they and the government will have to take account of the needs, wishes and views of patients and members of the public. The relationship between the government, the market and the public is delicately poised.

The government's journey beyond a monolithic top down NHS towards a devolved health service, offering wider choice and greater diversity is laudable. Its insistence on common standards, rigorous inspection and a willingness to draw on the professional values and aspirations of staff reduces the risk of harm. And, of course, this approach translates well to other public services.

It is people like Freddie Graham, his children and his granddaughter Jennifer who will need to be satisfied along the way. Freddie sees the logic of the current position, he still has a sense of fair play based on his own childhood but he is impatient for change and only time will tell if he and his even more demanding family (more Harry Potter than NHS specs) can be kept on board. As Freddie always says 'time is money in the financial services industry'.

References

DEPARTMENT OF HEALTH, 1996. *The National Health Service: A Service With Ambitions*. Presented to Parliament by the Secretary of State for Health.

DEPARTMENT OF HEALTH, 1998. *Information for Health*. Department of Health. London: Department of Health.

DEPARTMENT OF HEALTH, 2001. *Getting Ahead of the Curve: A Strategy for Combating Infectious Diseases by The Chief Medical Officer*. London: Department of Health.

DEPARTMENT OF HEALTH, 2002. *Delivering the NHS Plan*. London: Department of Health.

DEPARTMENT OF HEALTH, 2004. *Chief Executive's Report*. London: Department of Health. Gateway reference 3209.

Feachem, R.G.A., Sekhri, K., White, K.L., 2002, Getting more for their dollar: a comparison of the NHS with California's Kaiser Permanente, *BMJ*, 324 135-143.

Ferlie, E., Pettigrew, A., Ashburner, L., Fitzgerald, L., 1996, *The New Public Management in Action*. Oxford University Press ISBN 0 19 828902-2.

Griffiths, R., 1991. *Audit Commission Lecture*.

Hennessy, P., 1992, *Never Again – Britain 1945-1951*. London: Jonathan Cape ISBN 0 224 02768 9.

Hennessy, P., 2001, *Whitehall*. London: Pimlico ISBN 0712667555

Langlands, A., 2003, *Synchronising Higher Education and the NHS*, London: TSO ISBN 0 11 703218 2.

Le Grand, J., Propper, C., 1997, *Central Government and Quasi-Markets: The Case of Health Care*: London: LSE ISBN 0 7530 1333 9

Pettigrew, A.M., 1987, *Context and Action in the Transformation of the firm*. Journal of Management Studies 24:6: 0022-2380

Rowling, J.K., 1997, *Harry Potter and the Philosopher's Stone*, London: Bloomsbury, ISBN 07475 45723.

Singh, P.K., 2004, Effective Health Care: The role of government, market and civil society. World Health Organisation, Regional Health Forum WHO South East Asia Region (Vol. 6 No. 1).

THE INDEPENDENT COMMISSION ON GOOD GOVERNANCE IN PUBLIC SERVICES, 2004: *The Good Governance Standard for Public Services*, London: OPM & CIPFA ISBN 1 898531 86 2.

Timmins, N., 1995, *The Five Grants – A biography of the Welfare State*, London: Harper Collins ISBN 0 00 255388 0

Regulation

Sam Younger looks at the growth of 'independent' regulators, arguing that the way they relate to government makes them structurally weak. In an attempt to guarantee accountability, independence may be compromised.

Sam Younger

Sam Younger joined the Electoral Commission as its first Chairman after a career spanning twenty years at the BBC, most recently as Managing Director of BBC World Service from 1994–98. He was Chief Executive of the British Red Cross, responsible for its work both in the UK and around the world from 1999–2001. He is involved in a range of other activities including chairing the Quality Assurance Agency for Higher Education and chairing the governing body of the University of Sussex.

While having no personal history of party affiliation, politics runs in the family. His father was a Labour MP and Minister in the Labour Government of 1945–51, while more recently his cousin was a Cabinet Minister during Margaret Thatcher's Conservative administration.

The State as Regulator

"'You're not taking this seriously,' whispered her daemon. 'Behave yourself.'Her daemon's name was Pantalaimon, and he was currently in the form of a moth." Thus, on the opening page of his trilogy for children, *Northern Lights*, Philip Pullman introduces an imaginary world in which each character has a daemon. This takes many forms and acts both as helper and conscience. Without their daemons, the characters gradually cease to function.

Everyone needs their daemon, and they take many forms, ranging from individual conscience, through the moral pressures exerted by family and community to the rules imposed by professional groups and, ultimately, the coercive power of the state. The case for the state as regulator begins when individual conscience, social pressures or professional codes and organisations fail to guarantee the observation of standards of behaviour that society demands. In many areas, therefore, state regulation is uncontroversial, in principle if not always in its application. Laws against murder, rape, assault or theft – and the enforcement mechanisms that go with them – fall into this category. However, the state as regulator is more contentious when it deals with two issues: firstly, those where arguably the activities covered may be regarded as matters of individual conscience and choice in which the state has no business interfering – for example abortion; secondly, those areas in which there is a legitimate public interest but where some would argue "Let the market decide". The issues surrounding the state as regulator come into sharpest focus in the latter area.

The government's Better Regulation Task Force has defined regulation as "any measure or intervention that seeks to change the behaviour of individuals or groups". The underlying assumption is that, in areas of activity with a legitimate public interest, intervention to change behaviour is likely to be needed. Individuals or groups will tend to act in their own interest, to the potential detriment of others, in the absence of frameworks and processes that hold them to account, not because of malevolence but a human tendency to cut corners to achieve a goal, if you think you can get away with it. In my own management experience – for example on personnel issues, the reason to undergo due process rather than simply go ahead and do what I wanted to do was not my own conscience, but the awareness that I would be required to explain myself publicly and be held to account, in this case by trade union structures and procedures.

The demand for accountability has grown apace. This reflects fundamental changes in society: a move away from individuals needing to be protected against limitations on their freedom of action by the state to an emphasis on the rights of individuals to be guaranteed by the state – rights not just to security of life and limb but also to equality of treatment and, in many cases, equality and fairness of outcome. In its 2004 report on independent regulators, the House of Lords Committee on the Constitution pointed to three purposes of regulation: to compensate for "missing" markets, where the market does not operate; to compensate for market failure; and to change what would otherwise be unacceptable market outcomes. That is a very wide remit for potential regulatory activity and reflects the "consumerist" view. The job of the state is to ensure that the consumer is not just protected from exploitation but can also hold others to account for any outcomes not deemed acceptable.

As a result many bemoan the growth of the so-called "nanny state", which seeks to protect its citizens not just from unfair exploitation by others but also from their own mistakes and failures. The regulatory state risks drowning legitimate activity in bureaucracy and red tape; or worse still the state is given overweening power to force conformity with rules that stifle the freedom and enterprise of individuals and of society at large. That may be a loaded way of stating the issue, but it points to the importance of the state intervening as regulator sparingly and only where it can be demonstrated that society stands to benefit.

In an ideal world, professions and industries regulate themselves, maintaining standards to protect their collective reputation and provide reassurance to the public and consumer that their interests can be effectively safeguarded by the enlightened self-interest of the bodies concerned. Peer pressure and peer review should be the most effective and efficient form of regulation because they combine detailed understanding of the activity involved, a clear interest in protecting reputation and an interest in keeping the cost of regulation to a minimum. At the same time, the scrutiny by the public through politicians, the media and pressure groups should ensure that the public interest is kept in focus. Such champions of the public are quick to point the finger if they believe a self-regulating group is abusing its position or "protecting its own". Nevertheless the trend has been to move away from self-regulation towards some degree of independence in the regulatory framework, even where self-regulation remains the basic system. After all, few significant organisations – public or private – now rely entirely on themselves in their governance. Non-executive directors in public companies provide a measure of independence and scrutiny; many organisations in the public sector – for example universities – are required by their statutes to have a majority of independent members on their governing bodies, including an independent chair. That most fiercely self-regulating sector – the press – includes members from outside the profession on its Press Complaints Commission.

However, self-regulation encounters constant scepticism and the trend has been steadily towards independent statutory regulation in most areas of public life. The sceptical and often cynical spirit of the age tends to the belief that neither individuals nor groups can be relied upon to police themselves. Failures – whether through incompetence, negligence or intent – are no longer accepted as inevitable and unfortunate facts of life, but rather as evidence that the regulatory system does not adequately measure up to the task and needs to be strengthened. Areas where self-regulation exists are under growing pressure. An example is the General Medical Council and its response to Dame Janet Smith's enquiry into whether the General Medical Council was at fault in allowing Dr Harold Shipman to continue to practise and kill patients without detection. In her letter to the Home Secretary accompanying her fifth report, Dame Janet criticised the General Medical Council because "its procedures focused too much on the interests of the doctors and not sufficiently on the protection of patients". She went on: "I have concluded that there has not yet been the change of culture within the General Medical Council that will ensure that patient protection is given the priority it deserves. I have been driven to the conclusion that this is because the General Medical Council is effectively controlled by members elected by doctors. Many of the issues which the General Medical Council has to consider give rise to a conflict between the interests of the profession and the public interest. Many members of the profession expect the General Medical Council to represent it rather than regulate it in the public interest. One of my recommendations is that the number of members appointed against public interest criteria should be increased so that members elected by the medical profession no longer have an overall majority." The General Medical Council responded by saying that it had made and continued to bring forward changes to strengthen public involvement, but the pressures on the profession are unlikely to diminish.

Another area where self-regulation is under the microscope is the press, which for many years has appeared to be on the brink of being subjected to a statutory framework of regulation because, in the words used by David Mellor when he was the relevant Secretary of State – it was "drinking in the last chance saloon". The Press Complaints Commission is widely thought to have provided insufficient redress for those whose privacy has been invaded or whose reputations have been unfairly undermined by newspapers whose power and influence are far greater than their sense of public responsibility. Government has up to now shied away from statutory regulation partly because it would simply be too controversial but also on the substantive ground that the freedom of the press to investigate and expose wrongdoing is so fundamental a part of the fabric of a free society that it should not be compromised by statutory regulation that might protect the undeserving in its attempt to protect the deserving.

An analagous argument applies to the case of Members of Parliament. Concerns about standards of behaviour among MPs – fuelled, it should be said, by a very small number of 'causes celebres' – led in 1995 to the establishment of a Parliamentary Commissioner for Standards as an independent figure who would set standards and investigate complaints under the self-regulating auspices of the House of Commons Standards and Privileges Committee. This rather than external regulation is regarded by parliamentarians as critical to the maintenance of the independence of parliament as an institution, in much the same way as parliamentary privilege. Nevertheless, the injection of external elements into parliament's essentially self-regulatory system has remained on the agenda. An element of statutory regulation was introduced by the Political Parties Elections and Referendums Act 2000, which imposed a donations reporting requirement on MPs. More recently, the Committee on Standards in Public Life has recommended that for serious cases an Investigatory Panel should be set up and should include an independent legal Chair from outside the House of Commons – a proposal that has been resisted by parliament.

The clearest and most substantive danger in moving away from self-regulation to a statutory framework – or at least some statutory elements – lies in the possibility of influence by the government of the day. Although excessive bureaucracy is one concern, the crucial consideration is that the demands of the public interest should not be defined and implemented by the government through ministers. Hence the trend towards "independent" regulators. The rise of independent regulators can be seen as an attempt to reconcile the need for independence from government interference with the need for the public interest to be protected by something more robust than self-regulation. Government proposes and parliament debates, amends and enacts the statutory framework for regulation. However, once the framework is in place, an independent regulator should get on with the job free of political interference or control. "The creation, design and consequences of independent regulatory agencies represent a classic example of delegation to non-majoritarian institution", according to Mark Thatcher in *West European Politics* (2002). "They are created by legislation, hence elected officials are their principals. They are organisationally separate from governments and headed by unelected officials. They are given powers over regulation, but are also subject to controls by elected politicians and judges." A Better Regulation Task Force Report on independent regulators in 2003 listed a number of benefits of independent regulation identified by those subject to it – more consistency of decision-making; long-term decisions rather than short-term; more transparency; better accountability; more trust between the regulated and the regulator; and freedom from political interference. Those surveyed who were directly regulated all had complaints about their regulator; but nearly all preferred the independent regulator to control by a Whitehall department.

Nevertheless, there are limits to the model. Most independent regulators are linked to a government department. They are often described as part of the "quango state" and it is no coincidence that the acronym uses the phrase "quasi" autonomous, for they are not entirely independent. Ministers decide on appointments and – even where these are open to public competition – there can be suspicion of political motivation or patronage. Re-appointments may also be at ministerial discretion, although there is a growing trend toward single term appointments in order to eliminate the suspicion that incumbents will seek to make sure they do not offend the minister who may be responsible for their re-appointment. More important, government departments are responsible for setting the budgets of many independent regulators; and while there may not be any direct link between the decisions of a regulator and the budget approved, there may nevertheless be pressure to avoid antagonising government for fear of budgetary consequences. To say this is in no way to impugn the very real independence of those appointed to independent regulatory agencies; rather it is a structural weakness because, while the reporting line to a government department guarantees good accountability, it carries with it the risk that independence could be seen as circumscribed.

That is why the model represented by the Electoral Commission is interesting. Given the Commission's core statutory responsibility for regulating the financial affairs of political parties, from the outset it needed to be seen to be entirely independent of the government. Hence it was established with accountability not to a parent department, but directly to parliament through a specially created "Speaker's Committee". This committee approves the Commission's budget, and scrutinises it for value for money. Although the government is represented on the committee ex-officio by relevant ministers, it is an all-party body chaired by the Speaker and with no government majority. When it comes to appointments, these are made on a vote in the House of Commons on the recommendation of the Speaker. Thus independence from government is guaranteed to a greater extent than in the case of non-departmental public bodies. However, the opposite problem arises because the accountability mechanisms are not as well developed as they are for bodies which account to departments. This problem is compounded by the fact that, although a representative of the Speaker's Committee answers questions in parliament about the activities of the Commission, he or she does not speak on behalf of the Commission. Yet there is no other opportunity for parliamentary debate on the Commission's work because there is no government minister to introduce or answer a debate. Nonetheless, the model is worth pursuing and developing as a way of ensuring independence from government. At the same time, to be effective as a model, parliament would need to develop its own infrastructure to hold such bodies effectively to account. Independence should not result in a lack of accountability. By the same token, the other side of the coin of proper scrutiny by parliament is confidence in the organisation and hence the championing of its independent role if that is called into question.

If the framework within which independent statutory regulators work can be made to reflect a proper balance between independence and accountability; and if the state is inevitably going to continue to be required to provide for regulation in a wide range of areas – what makes a good regulator? Although the core priority is of course, within the statutory framework, to understand and champion the public interest, it seems to me that an equally important starting point is not just an understanding of but also a sympathy with the legitimate needs of the regulated. To be an effective regulator you need to want the people or bodies you are regulating to be successful because you regard the activity on which they are engaged to be important. Equally, the regulator's starting point should be the presumption that those regulated by and large possess no less integrity than the regulator and will – in the overwhelming majority of cases – wish to do the best possible job within the boundaries of the law and good practice. Indeed it is vitally important to ensure that the existence of an independent regulator does not lead to the regulated abdicating their own responsibility to implement and manage their own standards. The first responsibility for compliance and best practice rests within organisations themselves and their aim should be to make the regulator redundant. This was illustrated in the tenth report of the Committee on Standards in Public Life, in its analysis of the ethical standards framework for local government. The centralised system, it said "has arguably removed primary responsibility for standards from individual authorities (and members). Local Standards Committees, critical in our view to embedding high standards in each local authority, are under-used and in danger of falling into disrepair."

The first priority of the regulator should therefore be, as far as is compatible with the duties imposed by law, to leave the regulated to get on with the job. Secondly, the regulated have the right to as much clarity as possible as to what is expected of them. This is not always easy for the regulator since the laws passed by parliament may not always be clear; nor do they always anticipate issues that arise when they are applied. Nevertheless, clarity is vital and the goalposts must not be constantly shifting. Thirdly, the regulated will legitimately want to minimise the costs of compliance. This is not only a financial issue. It is also a matter of the culture that is established. The burden of regulation has to have the minimum possible impact on the willingness of those who are regulated to give of their best. In the case of the political parties, there is a feeling that the regulatory regime in place since 2001 has discouraged volunteers from coming forward to act as treasurers of local party organisations for fear of falling foul of the regulator – or more accurately the law. While much of this may be the result of the way the law is framed, it is important that the regulator do nothing to compound the problem. It is also of enormous importance to the regulated that reputation is not unnecessarily damaged. There is always a danger that a regulator's activity is seen as proof that the activities of the organisations being regulated are suspect and that the only thing saving them from themselves is the vigilance of the regulator. Regulators themselves can inadvertently fuel such views and need to recognise that reputation is as much the concern of the regulated as it is of the body to whose remit it may be more explicitly central.

This raises the issue of how regulators can ensure that they comprehend the perspective of the regulated. Should regulators be of the industry or sector they are regulating or should they stand outside it? The norm is a mixture of the two, perhaps with a majority of outsiders. Credibility demands that a regulator be able to demonstrate understanding of the industry. An editorial in the *Financial Times* (19th January 2005) on an enquiry into a tribunal involving the Financial Services Authority said that "the Financial Services Authority appears to have been more professional in its performance than the self-regulatory organisations that preceded it at the time when the mis-selling happened. However, it will have to become much more professional if it is to command the respect of the organisations it regulates". This is even more important for an organisation such as the Electoral Commission, because the law prevents anyone from being appointed as a Commissioner who has in the previous ten years been an elected member, candidate or office-holder of a registered political party. This has led to concerns that the Commission cannot adequately understand the political parties' perspective. There was a debate in parliament, when the Bill to establish the Commission was going through, about whether recently active politicians should be eligible to be Commissioners. The view that prevailed was that the Commission's independence was best served by not including politicians, but that the Commission would work with a Parliamentary Parties Panel to advise it.

Although in this case my view is that the arrangements put in place by parliament are right ones, the Commission needs to work intensively to ensure that it fully understands the party perspective. Nevertheless, the ability of the organisation to develop and sustain a reputation for impartiality is much enhanced by the absence of suspicion of a partisan perspective at the heart of its consideration. More generally, regulatory bodies must balance their ability to understand the needs and views of the regulated with an ability – however imperfect – to reflect a wider public interest.

Independence and impartiality, therefore, have to be balanced by a real understanding of the activities being regulated and a willingness consistently to engage and to listen. Equally, independence has to be balanced by accountability; consistency in the way in which regulation is applied is a key consideration but has to be balanced with a flexibility and a sense of proportionality. Behind these lie integrity and transparency – both of them essential to the credibility of any independent regulatory activity, though no more so than in other areas of public activity. Finally, and in many ways the most difficult of all to achieve, is the flexibility and tough-mindedness not to assume that the regulatory activity being undertaken now will necessarily be valid for all time. All organisations tend to want to defend the territory they occupy and if anything expand it rather than contemplate contraction. However, the state as regulator should be seeking to do as little rather than as much as possible. The Better Regulation Task Force, in championing Regulatory Impact Assessments and raising the possibility that new regulations should be balanced by the elimination of old ones, is pointing in the right direction. The balance, both in terms of the extent of regulation and the way in which it is implemented, will never be right – either in general or in particular. It can and should, though, be the subject of continuous debate and adjustment.

CHANGING **TIMES**

Trust, Accountability and Regulation

In *A View from "Near Abroad"* Baroness O'Neill calls for the development of intelligent forms of accountability, arguing that government and the civil service often confuse accountability with management and control.

Baroness Onora O'Neill CBE

Onora O'Neill is Principal of Newnham College, Cambridge. She writes on ethics and political philosophy, with particular interests in international justice, the philosophy of Immanuel Kant, questions of bioethics and conceptions of accountability and trust. She sits in the House of Lords as a crossbencher (Baroness O'Neill of Bengarve), chairs the Nuffield Foundation and is President-elect of the British Academy.

A View from "Near Abroad"

In Russia one hears the newly independent states that were once part of the former Soviet Union spoken of as "near abroad". The phrase might also be used to characterise those parts of the public sector that lie beyond the civil service. They are not part of the civil service, but they are not distant from it either. Those of us who work in the "near abroad" of the public sector (such as the universities) recognise – how could we not? – the huge and proper role of government, and therefore of the civil service, in determining what we may and may not do, what we must do, and how well we are funded. In many respects we are fortunate – unlike counterparts in certain other countries – in that we can take for granted that civil servants in the UK will act with propriety, and that we will not encounter either gross corruption or the demands of nepotists.

We are less sure that the civil service is well placed to tell us how to organise our primary activities. The largest public sector institutions provide highly complex and diverse services, in particular education and health care, to huge sections of the public. In these institutions there is a persistent sense that the government, and with it the civil service, regularly – if unintentionally – harm the work that has to be done by requiring that it be organised in ways that are often poorly chosen for the tasks at hand. This unease is often expressed piecemeal in grumbles about red tape or about excessive demands for recording and providing information that is poorly related to tasks; in resentment of change, of too much change, or of too rapid change; in comments on underfunding, or on terms and conditions of work. But for many who work in public sector institutions these are not the central concerns. The underlying worry is that government, acting through the civil service, too often imposes policies that damage or compromise the possibility of doing primary tasks well, and thereby the likelihood of delivering a good service to members of the public.

Of course, those who make the charge may be self-serving or reluctant to be held to account – at least this accusation is common enough, and I have often heard it made by those who defend government policies, and by civil servants. They suggest that the grumbles and the unease cloak nostalgic and illegitimate hankerings for a (perhaps mythical) world in which hospitals were run for the convenience of consultants, universities for the convenience of dons and schools for the convenience of teachers, and so on.

If this sort of self-interest were the sole explanation of persistent unease, it could be quickly dismissed. Since the public sector is funded by public money and delivers services to the public, accountability for the use of funds and for quality of provision is uncontroversial. But this is the typical reason, and it is certainly not a good reason, for misgivings where demands are poorly connected to, and sometimes destructive of, the work that actually has to be done in the various parts of the public sector. Chagrin about being held accountable by ill-designed methods, that in the worst cases damage the work that has to be done, is not a matter of resistance to being held to account. What is needed in the "near abroad" of the public sector is not removal of accountability, but a shift to more intelligent forms of accountability.

2. Managing or holding to account?

The civil service – rightly – takes management seriously. Its focus on delivery of services, on value for money and on communicating information to the public is not in itself controversial. Where the civil service manages delivery of services, a commitment to managing them well is important: here discussions of targets and effective and efficient delivery is in place. But where the civil service does not in fact manage or deliver services to the public, and the task of managing falls on others, the civil service's task is to hold those others to account for their use of public funds and for the quality of the services they deliver.

In the corporate sector there is a clear understanding that management is not the same as accountability. First, management is downwards, but accountability is upwards. The CEO of a company manages the company and its employees, but is accountable upwards to the board and with them to shareholders (and sometimes to regulators: another topic). Second, management is first-order and focused on performance of primary tasks, but accountability is second-order and focused on judging (reports of) performance or non-performance of primary tasks. Management addresses primary tasks, in particular the delivery of products or services, and is typically done by setting targets that are relevant to the tasks to be achieved, and by rewarding good and penalising poor performance. Accountability is a matter of holding those who carry primary tasks to account by judging what has been done – or not done! – relying on independent auditors, inspectors, and examiners where required or relevant. Third, and consequently, management is prospective, but accountability is retrospective. Fourth, the sanctions used in managing and holding to account differ. Sanction for failure to manage performance well may include loss of employment and falling revenue. At a later stage when those who carried – or failed to carry – the primary tasks are held to account a second range of sanctions may follow; failure may lead to falling share prices, changes in the boardroom, even take-over or bankruptcy; success may lead to rising share prices, company growth (and personal rewards for managers).

In short, management in the private sector is indeed a matter of command and control, and comes in harder or softer versions; but accountability is a matter of corporate governance, and is not managerially structured. The structures needed for managerial grip are not the same as those needed to ensure accountability, and accountability is not achieved by imposing a second layer of distance management.

Yet across the last twenty years the distinction between management and accountability has been increasingly blurred for those working in the public sector. The blurring is particularly evident in the big public sector institutions such as the NHS, schools and universities. All are assured that they must manage themselves, and that they are not managed from, but are rather accountable to, Whitehall. Yet the ways in which funding is provided, in which targets are set, in which information is required, in which performance is measured and monitored in abstraction from primary tasks, and sanctions are organised, often converge with and become indistinguishable from management from afar.

The big public sector institutions employ very many people and produce complex and differentiated ranges of services for large numbers of patients, pupils, students and other 'clients'. Many of their structures are complex, many of their tasks are long term and intricate, many of their objectives and outputs are incommensurable (there is no common 'unit of value', as there is in the corporate sector). The governance of these institutions is typically designed to take account of the long term balancing of multiple tasks and the retention and motivation of highly specialised employees. Most of the workforce is not mainly engaged in administration or management, and must be protected from the excessive clerical and managerial demands that tend to proliferate when the aim is management at a distance. The systems needed for these institutions and their work forces to be held to account need to take intelligent account of the nature of the work that is to be done. This requires intelligent and substantive focus on the tasks to be done. It cannot be done by concentrating on selected 'indicators' of performance devised primarily for managerial purposes.

Both health and education offer vivid – indeed notorious – examples of the ill effects of managing from afar rather than holding to account. For example, secondary school examinations have been distorted over many years by creating excessive incentives to ensure that more and more pupils obtain the magic 5 GCSE passes with grades of C or better. This creates pressing reasons to enter pupils for examination in the subjects in which they are most likely to get A to C grades. The bizarre, yet predictable, result of schools and pupils 'gaming' the system has been that while half of the age cohort now obtain the 5 desired passes, only a third obtain them in the three required subjects of English, Maths and

Science. The A to C grades are easier to get in subjects that are judged less central – and that matter less to future employers. Here conflating management with accountability has distorted education.

Meanwhile – in other rooms in the same department of state – somebody set a target for 50% of the age cohort to go to university, without apparently noting that two thirds of the age cohort do not reach a satisfactory standard in English, Maths and Science at age 16. At a later date – perhaps in yet another room in the same department – the circle was squared by putting forward legislation that gives universities an additional regulator to ensure that they improve 'access' for underrepresented groups in order to achieve this target.[1] Nobody has yet explained to the universities how they are to bring the approximately 16% of the age cohort who did not even get C's in the core subjects at GCSE to degree standard in *any* subject, traditional or modern, academic or vocational.[2]

An equally well-known range of examples emanated from another department of state that identified waiting times for non-urgent surgery as a key performance indicator for the NHS. Excessive stress on one output in a complex system led to inventive scheduling and recording of 'patient journeys', and to other 'unintended' consequences of institutions 'gaming' a system. Yet enthusiasm for distance management has not been extinguished by this experience. The same department of state recently brought forward legislation to reorganise the management of all human tissues that would have made the work of pathologists virtually impossible. Fortunately the *Human Tissues Act 2004* was massively altered during its passage through parliament, but the Act leaves a confusing and still indeterminate set of requirements for pathology services, and a daunting task for the Human Tissues Authority that is to sort matters out. In this case a massively disproportionate response to the careless and offensive (but not criminal) use of tissues at Alder Hey Hospital was taken as reason for detailed rewriting of the rule book in ways that would change the management of all pathology services. There was indeed good reason to legislate to prevent the too casual subsequent research use of the very small number of tissues lawfully removed *post mortem* under Coroner's authority: but this special case did not provide a good starting point for devising extremely detailed rules for managing the custody and use of the vastly greater number of tissue specimens taken from the living for the care of the living.

3. Better regulation?

It may be said – in fact, it is very often said – that such examples are either dated or (if recent) anomalous. Supposedly we are now well into an era of 'lighter touch' regulation, and these examples are remnants of a culture of control that was once needed – or at least thought to be needed – but is now on the way out. The glass of regulatory excess is supposedly emptying, although the pessimists in the public sector go on complaining that it is overflowing. The picture, in fact, is one of sporadic change, but far from reassuring.

Although there may be some genuine shift in the degree to which schools are managed from afar there is a mixed picture of change in the degree to which government and civil service still seek to manage higher education from afar. On the positive side, the realities of 'hyper-regulation'[3] have at least been widely noted and documented since 2000. For example, in 2000 the Higher Education Funding Council for England published a report, *Better Accountability for Higher Education*.[4] It pointed to uncoordinated, duplicated and redundant arrangements, and ascribed this variously to the diversity of univerity governance and to lack of communication and trust between universities and 'stakeholders'. It also noted that the higher education sector was one of low risk, so hardly in need of hyper-regulation.

A similar picture emerges from the work of the Better Regulation Task Force, established in 1997. The task force bases its work on "five Principles of Good Regulation" (identified as Proportionality, Accountability, Consistency, Transparency, Targeting). It has published a number of trenchant reviews of the impact of excessive and intrusive regulation, including the encouragingly titled *Higher Education: Easing the Burden*,[5] to which government responded positively.[6] Some welcome changes occurred. Nevertheless, the *Higher Education Act 2004* introduced two new regulators for universities (the Office of Fair Access and the Office of the Independent Adjudicator). A short browse of the Higher Education Funding Council for England's website shows that control remains very detailed. Other examples would show a similarly mixed picture of recognition of the costs of inflated structures for accountability into forms of management from afar, coupled with continued reliance on that approach. Any doubts that managerialism rather than lighter touch approaches to accountability are still the dominant approaches to holding public sector institutions to account can be removed by visiting the Department for Education and Skills and Department of Health websites (augmented by a brisk visit to the Higher Education Funding Council for England's website for those still unconvinced).

At present there is a wide gap between acknowledgement – by government, by the Better Regulation Task Force, by civil servants – of the impact of hyper-regulation on the public sector, and the realities on the ground. Fortunately the Better Regulation Task Force have not given up, and in March 2005 published a report to the Prime Minster, *Regulation   Less is More: Reducing Burdens, Improving Outcomes*, in which they recommend the Dutch system of setting targets for the reduction of administrative burdens on business, and propose a 'one in, one out' process for controlling the tendency of regulation to accumulate (the Irish used to use a 'one in, two out' system for reducing the number of licences to sell alcohol: perhaps worth a thought?). It would be encouraging to see this approach used in holding the public sector to account. Yet anybody who watches the massive quantity of new regulation and 'guidance' that is constantly issued, the minimal attention to reducing existing requirements, and the minimal amount of consolidated legislation, knows that change is glacially slow even when intentions are good.

4. Some sources of hyper-regulation

Many different views are offered about the emergence of the culture of hyper-regulation – or, as I have argued, of distance management masquerading as accountability – in the UK. One of its sources, it seems to me, may be a persistent confusion of management, accountability and regulation. This conflation is found even in the work of those most committed to improving the current situation. In its discussion of principles the Better Regulation Task Force starts from the thought that "Regulation may widely be defined as any government measure or intervention that seeks to change the behaviour of individuals or groups".[7] By this generous – not to say sloppy – standard *everything* from central planning to reporting requirements, from legislation to guidance, from direct management to second-order systems of accountability, will count as regulation. Indeed, suitably used forms of encouragement and reliable patterns of corruption would also have to count as regulation! Choices of terminology may not matter much; but obliterating significant distinctions can matter a lot. In taking so generous a view of regulation, many issues and roles are blurred. In my view, a lot of the difficulties faced by the public sector arise from an assumption that since government, and thereby the civil service, fund the public sector and initiate legislation, thereby writing the basic rules for the "near abroad" parts of the public sector, they must not only hold to account but control and manage its delivery of services.

The experiment of managing the public sector from the centre has of course been tried in many states; its pure form is known as central planning. But this is not ostensibly what is aimed at in the UK. Ostensibly the civil service manages delivery of services only when it does so directly, or through an agency – for example the payment of benefits, issuing passports or driving licences. But in other areas public services are managed and delivered by other relatively autonomous institutions, such as NHS trusts, schools or universities. There would be little disagreement that these public sector institutions should be accountable to government, and through them to the public, and that the civil service should play a crucial role in implementing accountability. But there would be a great deal of disagreement with the view that this is best done by micro-management from afar. Intelligent accountability is not a matter of micro-management from afar, but of ensuring informed and independent scrutiny of performance.

5. Some limits of transparency

The relationship of the executive – ministers and civil servants alike – to the more autonomous parts of the public sector has traditionally not been seen as managerial. Traditionally governments and civil servants draft the rulebooks for the public sector, which are then amended and enacted by parliament. Since they provide funding they subsequently hold to account both for expenditure of public funds and for compliance with the rulebook. But they have not traditionally managed in detail. It is not immediately obvious why they should wish to do so, or why they should not find it preferable to hold to account.

Indeed the present system has created large difficulties for government and for the civil servants. By taking increasing control of the delivery of public services, governments become accountable to the electorate for delivery of those services. A poor school cannot now be blamed on a dysfunctional Local Education Authority or an aberrant head teacher. Every failure in a school or hospital is liable to be seen as a case of government failure, of government missing its targets, or failing to improve public services. Both opposition parties and the media are quick to point the finger. Government is hoist by its own petard. It is now blamed for crowded waiting rooms, poor school discipline (and meals!) and for delayed operations. The system may not be one of central planning, but it has become one in which failure at any point in the public services is blamed on government – although they ostensibly to do not manage the services that failed. No wonder that those who take the blame seek to reduce the problem by constantly altering and adding to the ways in which they control those who actually deliver services. There is some irony in this outcome.

These changes have many sources, but one is evidently the increasing demand for transparency, which is intended to ensure that the public can judge the public services they receive. Transparency is now enshrined not merely in Freedom of Information legislation, but in the Nolan Principles for Conduct in Public life and in the Better Regulation Task Force's five principles of better regulation. It is said to be the key to making information, including information about quality of services delivered, about financial probity and about value for money available not only to those who understand the details, but to those who do not. Transparency is the antithesis of secrecy or obscurity, as a matter of bringing information out into the open where anybody may judge it.

There are not many critics of transparency these days. I think this is a pity, since it is a defective ideal. Transparency requires information to be made available – but it does not require that information be communicated in ways that are accessible to and useful for particular audiences. Good communication has to be audience sensitive: mere transparency can shirk this demand. Like the related ideals of disclosure, dissemination and self-expression, transparency does not demand good or honest communication with specific audiences – or any audience. It is generally achieved by putting government documents (long, prolix and seldom thrilling) onto departmental websites, which is useful for specialists, and by disseminating limited tabular information that looks disarmingly simple, yet cannot be properly interpreted without considerable expertise.

Many of the managerial demands placed on the public sector have the secondary purpose of securing transparency by generating information that can be published for the public at large, or for groups of 'stakeholders'. 'Simplified' comparative information about the performance of hospitals, schools and universities is compiled and published in the tabular form, usually in the form of league tables. Anybody can see who comes top or bottom, and the need for communicating information to wider audiences is supposedly satisfied.

However not everybody can see behind these simplified tables and rankings, or interpret their significance. Evaluating the performance of a pupil or a school in the round is quite difficult. School reports on individual pupils and inspectors' reports on schools are generally more useful for this task. In the end judging the quality of a university course or a student's work, of a hospital or an individual doctor, is probably not best achieved by league tables. Indeed, league tables are not designed to reveal quality of performance, but at most to compare and rank quality of performance. In some areas even those who come top may be performing at a mediocre level, in others those who do worst may perform satisfactorily. All this is well known, and those who deal with league tables are conscious of the pitfalls. However the wider public with less time and less expertise may be less aware of these arcane matters.

Communication with the public and with 'stakeholders' is important in democracies, but it is unlikely that transparency will be enough for high quality communication. These limitations have been recognised to a degree in the Education Bill before parliament in 2005 which aims to reinforce and simplify the inspection regime and to rely on a 'single conversation' rather than a portfolio of initiatives to drive school improvement.[8] Conversation, narrative and plain English directed at specific audiences for specific purposes, is more likely to achieve honest communication with particular 'stakeholders' – and with the wider public. So there are signs of hope as well as grounds for worry: too often the word from Whitehall is that changes are now agreed, and the experience in the public sector is that they are pretty distant.

Nor should we underestimate how difficult it is to communicate well about complex matters. In another essay in this volume, John Lloyd points out that providing information for the public at large used to be a task for the media. He reminds us that: "In a genuinely free society, the media's civic role should rather be to assist the people of that society to understand all kinds of powers – state, corporate, associative, cultural, foreign – so they, the people, can hold them to account through their actions, chief among which must be voting and other participation in civic life."

Unfortunately large parts of the media have abandoned this role, and the contribution to democracy that it makes. Where the media do not report systematically to citizens, it is tempting for government to insist that the civil service take over the task. But if they are to take on this task, it cannot be reduced to transparency, any more than holding to account can be conflated with quasi-management from afar.

Notes

1. The Regulator is the *Office of Fair Access* (OFFA), established under the *Higher Education Act 2004*.

2. The received answer to those who voice this wonder is that it is not a problem since the target is for 50% to get there *by age thirty* – whether by endless retakes or by dropping standards remains unclear.

3. I adapt the phrase from the title of Michael Moran's *The British Regulatory State: High Modernism and Hyper-innovation* Oxford University Press, 2003.

4. http://www.hefce.ac.uk/Pubs/Hefce/2000/00_36.pdf

5. *Higher Education: Easing the Burden*, BRTF, 2003.
   http://www.brtf.gov.uk/reports/highedentry.asp

6. http://www.brtf.gov.uk/responses_new/highered.asp

7. http://www.brtf.gov.uk/docs/pdf/principlesleaflet.pdf

8. The Bill reflects *A New Relationship with Schools*, published jointly by the Government and Ofsted in June 2004; see http://www.ofsted.gov.uk/publications/

CHANGING **TIMES**

Media, Politics and Government Communication

John Lloyd looks at the growth of the media and subsequent change in the balance of power between journalists, broadcasters and politicians, arguing that proper debate in a free society requires a rational public space, not a war zone.

In *Media and Politics* Howell James says that the challenges for government communication are more exacting than ever. A wider, more ambitious remit for government communication is required; one which retains the core civil service values of honesty and impartiality.

John Lloyd

John Lloyd is the Editor of *FT Magazine.* Earlier work with the *Financial Times* included as Industrial Editor, East European Editor and Moscow Bureau Chief.

He also writes for *Prospect*, *Toronto Globe* and *Mail*, and *Les Echos*. He is a member of the Advisory Board of the Moscow School of Political Studies.

Books include *Loss without Limit: The British Miners' Strike* (1985), *Rebirth of a Nation: An Anatomy of Russia* (1998) and *What the Media are doing to our politics* (June 2004).

The Media and Politics

Broadcasters sometimes like to show clips from old TV newsreels, culled from the 1940s or 50s, of BBC reporters waiting deferentially for the Prime Minister to disembark from a plane or a car, to ask him when he does   'have you anything to say to the BBC, Prime Minister?' What these clips show is an assumption of half a century ago: the assumption that political power trumped all others. Now it doesn't: media power comes closer to trumping all others – at least in some things. It is the power of the media which has been one of the largest shifts in society over the past three decades: it may come to be seen as the single most important trend in the conduct of politics in Britain.

For broadcasters, a high water mark of the independence they gained from the political sphere was an interview, in the autumn of 1982, between the late Sir Robin Day and Sir John Nott, then the Defence Secretary. The interview, conducted during the Falklands War, was testy: at one point, Day asked why he and the TV audience should believe what Nott said – since he was 'a transient, here-today, and if I may say so, gone-tomorrow politician'. Nott tore off his microphone, and left the studio.

The incident is celebrated, and was recalled by all of the obituaries on Day's death in 2000. Indeed, Nott himself called his memoir *Here Today, Gone Tomorrow*, observing on its publication in 2003 that the interview 'would be the only thing anyone remembered about me' – a prediction which is likely to be true. Indeed, the fact that he chose the phrase as a title was itself awry, or resentful.

It was a vivid mark of the change. For broadcasters and journalists, it was a change from deference, even servility, to a more challenging and equal relationship: a change which many politicians, especially those of the same generation or younger than the media radicals of the 50s and 60s, approved. The old order had seemed hidebound, stuffy and arrogant. The rule that matters which were due for debate in parliament in the following two weeks could not be commented on in the news media – defended by Winston Churchill during his last period as Prime Minister, saying that it would be 'shocking to have debates in this House forestalled, time after time, by expressions of opinion by persons who had not the status or responsibilities of MPs' – went in 1956, during the Suez crisis. Thereafter the status of parliament, as measured by the coverage it received, declined inexorably.

If newspapers have been part of this change, television has driven it – and driven newspapers. In a perceptive essay in 1998, Peter Riddell, the assistant editor (politics) of *The Times* wrote that 'the steady growth of current affairs programmes on television and radio since the late 1950s has provided a more direct way for leading politicians to communicate with the public. News is now a continuous 24-hour a day phenomenon, rather than one determined by the deadlines of the morning and evening papers. Politicians have responded. What is said on the *Today* programme often dominates the early editions of the *Evening Standard* and is then taken up in the lunchtime bulletins, all before parliament has begun sitting for the day'. Riddell quotes Jack Straw, the Foreign Secretary, complaining (in a Fabian pamphlet of 1992 which charted the steady drop in parliamentary reporting in broadsheet papers over the past 60 years) that 'the decline in press coverage of parliament must have a serious effect on the public's understanding of our democratic system'.

The pre-emption of parliament by television began happening when TV began to come of age, in the early sixties. One of the reasons President Kennedy is still regarded with such favour by the sixties generation which now runs things is because he was the first TV president: in his marvellous book, *The Powers that Be*, David Halberstam writes that 'in no way could Kennedy have been elected without television. It was that simple. He meshed politics and television with such charm and style and despatch that the intellectual elite of the country, which might normally have regarded the cross blend with trepidation, rich as it was in the potential for demagoguery, enthusiastically applauded him (in large part because the alternative to Kennedy was Richard M Nixon). Television loved him, he and the camera were born for each other, he was the first great political superstar; as he made television bigger, it made him bigger. Everyone using everyone. The media using the President, the President using the media'.

Kennedy made the first Faustian bargain of the TV age in politics. He brought TV in to take the place of parties and smoke filled rooms and deals and compromises among the old powers that were. And he made performance on TV the standard of future politicians, whether they liked it or not. His celebrated debate with Nixon helped establish him not just as the leading politician of his age, but established TV as the leading political arbiter of the age. That happened because of the technological innovation of the cathode ray tube, and because of the rapid expansion of television ownership and reception in homes in all rich countries from the early 1950s onwards: once that had happened, and that gave virtual but more or less instant access by millions to the deliberations of their representatives, all that has happened since had the air of inevitability.

The media took more power because they controlled access to the public – a public which they call an audience and the politicians call electors. The end of deference, celebrated so uncritically, was also the end of a shared assumption of supreme parliamentary sovereignty on the part of the political class, the media and the public. While that remains true as a statement of constitutional fact, day to day 'sovereignty' has bit by bit passed to the media – in the sense that they dictate, or strongly influence, the political rhythm, the nature of the debate, the choice and saliency of issues, the style of questioning, the prominence or obscurity of public figures, the framing of these figures in a harsh or kindly light and the amount of news, analysis and debate broadcast, compared with entertainment. It has changed enormously the set of skills needed to be a politician: Professor Jean Seaton observes that 'the definition of political leadership depends, to an extraordinary extent, on the capacity of a politician for self-projection on the screen'. A comparison between the careers of Tony Blair and Ian Duncan-Smith makes the point strongly: though the capacity for 'self projection on the screen' was not the only difference between their relative abilities, it was a critically important one.

Journalism is terribly important: more important, ironically, than we have allowed. It is part of a great power, which is the media: and they make up, below the state, the greatest aggregation of power in the land. When the late Anthony Sampson published his *Who Runs this Place* last year – the last version of his famous 'Anatomy of Britain' series, which stretched over 40 years of pioneering work and was, unfortunately, his last book – he remarked that of all the powers which had waxed and waned in the close to half century between the first book and the most recent, that which had waxed everyone else off the map was the power of the media. He wrote – 'the masters of the media are the new aristocracy, demanding and receiving homage from politicians, big businessmen and the aristocracy…columnists and broadcasters are more famous than the politicians or public figures they interview; they know they can make or break reputations and ruin political careers.'

They have become so great, as Sampson makes clear, because other powers have waned. Those institutions in which people put their faith and trust – organised Christian religion, political parties, parliament, trades unions, associations of all kinds, the nation as an object of patriotic fervour and devotion, the family and authority figures – all declined in favour. The media, and the state, increased its power and scope, the former very greatly indeed. The amount of time given over to media, especially broadcast media, rose to between four or five hours a day on average – by far the largest single call on peoples' leisure time.

What had been a largely dependent relationship of the news media on politics and the state (at least until the emergence of powerful and profitable newspapers in the mid-19th century, and in many societies long after that – indeed, in many, even now) has in wealthy democratic states become one of dependence in the other direction. Politicians had kept papers going financially, dictated their policies and shut them off from their sources of information, even from their public, at will. The situation is not wholly reversed, but it is partially so. The new institutions of the media, which emerged fully from the 1920s, first of all in the US – a powerful set of newspapers independent of parties and the state practising aggressive and often oppositional journalism, a popular film production in most advanced countries but with its headquarters in Hollywood and broadcasting companies which were increasingly independent of the state even when the state raised their income – meant that media became, as Paul Starr writes, 'an independent factor in politics – no less important… than the political parties which once held sway over them'.

The power of the media is insisted on here because it has become so pervasive as to be taken for granted – at least by the general public, if not by politicians and other public figures who are the frequent objects of their attention. And for another reason: the effect of the media on political life. Political parties and governments have framed their policies, programmes and practices round the media – because they have believed that they have had little choice. In an environment where large powers control information, access and mood, politicians who wish to be effective have two choices: to rail against what they see as the iniquities of media power and its abuse; or to come to a series of deals with the powers-that-be (as Halberstam called them) and hope that these deals hold sufficiently for them to be able to get policies across and avoid too many scandals, revelations and denunciations which are the inevitable concomitants of dominant and scandalously-inclined media. Railing against the media is seen, by leaders of all parties, as a losers' strategy: it was that practised by Neil Kinnock, when leader of the Labour Party. Kinnock's evisceration by (especially) the right-wing tabloids was deeply unfair, highly politically motivated and often mendacious: his mistake was to point that out. The common, if unstated agreement among all politicians since then, has been that the media should not be confronted: they are simply too powerful.

Media power has not ushered in a nightmare. The BBC remains committed to a large output of public service journalism of different sorts – the more necessary, as commercial TV drops nearly all of its current affairs output, and keeps news as short as possible: to a lesser extent, the same is true of Channel Four. Radio is now very diverse, and through talk radio, has put on air large numbers of the public who take part in a vast conversation which covers an extraordinary wide range of areas: while BBC Radios Three and Four preserve a news, current affairs, arts and music output of uniquely high quality. Newspapers have a higher penetration than in any other major country other than Japan, and a few of them are very good by any international standards. If journalism can and does abuse its power, it can also use it for enlightenment, revelation, analysis and the provision of constant, relatively accurate, information. More, it increasingly calls for, and gets, displays of great courage – from Veronica Guerin's confrontation with Dublin drugs mafia through to the boldness of correspondents of all countries in Iraq to the stunning bravery of Sumi Khan, in Bangladesh, insulted, beaten and stabbed for articles alleging the involvement of political and religious leaders in violence against minorities, who lives and works still and – when honoured in the Index on Censorship awards in London – said that 'as long as I am alive, I will keep on working'. Journalism can be magnificent, especially in adversity: it can be destructive in power.

The media are the first to point out, and rightly, that power needs to be held to account. And thus media power itself needs to be examined, debated and argued over: above all, its effects for good and ill have to be understood as far as possible, and a debate begun on that. If – as most of those who have examined the media and society over the past century believe – they are the largest single example of a growing centre of authority, then they are open to an examination more searching than they have so far received from themselves, from the academy and from the public. The fact that the largest part of the media are private corporations and that there is an accepted convention that they are and should remain as independent as possible from the state does not cancel out the need for a more informed narrative about their power. The news media lay claim to a democratic as well as a commercial tradition: they say, and they are right to say, that they are essential to the creation and preservation of a democratic state. Where democracy is relatively healthy and civil society plural and diverse, free media flourish: the more the first two of these are absent or suppressed, the more suppressed the media tend to be – in an almost mechanical relationship (Russia and Zimbabwe are good cases in point where relatively free media are being squeezed down – in the latter's case, almost squeezed out). Since the media make that claim and society as a whole accepts it, their own health, practices, accuracy and ability to carry differing views are thus an urgent and central concern of society.

In considering the formula of 'holding power to account', the media might consider reframing it, so that it is better understood in a slightly changed form. In a genuinely free society, media's civic role should rather be to assist the people of that society to understand all kinds of powers – state, corporate, associative, cultural, foreign – so they, the people, can hold them to account through their actions, chief among which must be voting and other participation in civic life.

Change in the media is constant and rapid: but change is presently probably more intense than at any time in the recent past.

Regulation of broadcasting, the dominant medium for news and current affairs, is now at the centre of attention. The trend in most countries, led by the US, is for regulation's hand to be lighter and lighter. In the UK as elsewhere, the move away from prescribing blocks of time dedicated to news, current affairs, the arts and discussion has been greatly strengthened by the availability of satellite and digital channel. When the UK completes a switchover to digital-only signals by 2012 or thereabouts a point will be reached when – according to Stephen Carter, head of the regulator Ofcom, speaking in March this year – 'the old assumptions of public service broadcasting will be rendered unsustainable: by the end of switchover, Independent TV will be almost entirely free to do what it likes.' 'Doing what it likes' will mean – it's assumed – becoming more 'consumerist': that is, putting on programmes that the highest number of people like, as much of the time as possible.

Spectrum scarcity made possible the more-or-less explicit deal between state and broadcasters: that they provide public service programmes in return for the licence to broadcast. That deal was wholly or partly responsible for such programmes as World In Action, This Week, Weekend World (all gone) and the South Bank Show (still broadcasting). Its collapse puts all of the attention on the BBC: which will be torn between fulfilling a public service mandate, and competing with a 'liberated' independent sector as well as a host of digital and satellite channels. How Ofcom, and the government and parliament, and the public at large redefines the public service commitment in the next few years will be critical to the shape of both broadcasting, and of public life.

Both news providers and broadcasters are working with technologies which will allow them to deliver 'personalised' news and information services, especially to hand-held devices. The latter are seen as the largest growth area in the immediate future: and the new technologies allow news and information providers to send messages to customers with the accent on their interests, with advertisements aimed at the segments of the market in which they are known to be interested and with news 'scraped' from a multitude of sources which are tailored for their specific concerns. The notion of general news – whether in a newspaper or a TV or radio bulletin – will gradually be replaced by news which is composed by the individual customers' preferences: a future already being rehearsed in the present, and one likely to demand a radical reworking of both the ways in which news is packaged, and the ways in which it's paid for.

Weblogs, or blogs, are now growing at an exponential rate, and are seen by the burgeoning population of the 'blogging community' as a new kind of journalism – even, a new kind of relationship with power. The most highly publicised triumphs of this community are the political and media scalps – US Senator Trent Lott, outed in 2002 for racist comments at an appreciation ceremony for Strom Thurmond; the CBS news anchorman Dan Rather, whose 40-year career in the company was cut short last year by bloggers spotting that documents used in a newscast to show that President George W Bush had shirked his Texas Air National Guard duty with the connivance of his superiors were probably forged; and CNN news director Eason Jordan, forced to resign after a blogger revealed that he'd said, in an off-the-record speech at Davos this year, that US forces were deliberately targeting journalists. But the even greater importance of blogs is that they allow vast numbers of networks of conversation to take place and proliferate – many of which subvert established hierarchics, as the weblogs which are used by US soldiers and officers in the Iraq war, on which they post tips, experiences and vital information, so that the experienced sergeant is giving advice to the inexperienced colonel. This kind of 'subversion' will, in different ways, go on at all levels and in diverse places.

Newspapers will be one of these places. There is presently some anxiety within the newspaper world about whether or not they will survive, or at least in what form they will survive. The challenges of free newspapers, blogs, the internet, huge (and more individualised) choice in broadcast channels as well as rising generations which, for these and other reasons, aren't being converted to newspaper reading are all seen as signs that newspapers have to change dramatically. It is, however, unclear how that change will be managed – or if it can be successful. At the heart of these concerns is the question of news and its complexity: how to mobilise the resources for long, complex and expensive news gathering?

However that may turn out, the tabloids – at least in Britain – have probably had, and are still having, a more powerful effect on effect on the presentation and scope of news than any other single force. The tabloidisation of news – which works at a number of levels, most obviously infusing politics with an approach which privileges scandal and confrontation – is far advanced. For those who need high grade, complex and detailed information, specialised publications and programmes will be produced. We may be seeing the emergence of a highly differentiated marketplace in news and information which Jean Seaton describes as 'a growing voluntary apartheid here which did not previously exist, and one with alarming implications for our democracy: the gap between richest and poorest, employed and unemployed, educated and uneducated, may come to be measured not just by differences in health and opportunities but by an increasing polarisation of degrees of knowledge and understanding of current issues and political debates.'

A debate on and within the media is now running, at a higher level than in the recent past. This is partly because of the developments above: also because some journalists have felt alarm at the power of the media and the possibility – and the reality – of abuse, in both senses of the word; and because politicians have begun to query whether or not bending with the media wind is the only posture to be taken. Straws in that wind: the MP Peter Bradley has put forward, in the form of a 'Right of Reply and Press Standards' draft, a private members bill which would legislate for a statutory right of reply. Douglas Alexander, the Trade Minister, has written in a pamphlet for the Smith Institute, that 'we are witnessing the Oprahfication of politics. The growth of infotainment has seen boundaries between politics and entertainment become blurred. Politics as reported becomes a question of who's up and who's down, rather than being seen as the site of political choices'. Some leading politicians, such as John Reid and Charles Clarke, have been openly critical of a culture of aggression.

There is an opening for a wider and more profound reflection on the media's effect on politics and the public sphere – one which might lead to, or even proceed from, a realisation that the media and politics in free societies need a rational public space in which debate takes place: and that that space can be badly damaged by warfare.

Howell James CBE

Howell James started his working life in the media as head of promotions at Capital Radio. He was head of publicity at the launch of TVam, Britain's first commercial breakfast television channel. In 1984 he was appointed Special Adviser at the Cabinet Office, and from 1984–1987 he worked in the Department of Employment and the Department of Trade and Industry. In 1987 he joined the BBC as Director of Corporate Affairs and was a member of the BBC's Board of Management.

He joined Cable & Wireless as Director of Corporate and Government Affairs in 1992 where he was responsible for Cable & Wireless's press, public and government relations in the UK, North America and Hong Kong. Howell became Political Secretary to the PM in 1994 and worked in No 10 until 1997. He was a Founding Partner and Director of Brown Lloyd James, a corporate PR Company from 1997–2004. He became Permanent Secretary, Government Communication in July 2004. He was awarded the CBE in August 1997.

The Age of Explanation

"It must be remembered, also, that the newly appointed Labour Ministers had also new information officers to advise them; it was like the raw recruit and the unbroken horse – they had to learn together and some mistakes were inevitable. For example... on one occasion Central Office of Information government speakers were briefed with a handout from the Labour Party Headquarters."

Not, as some might imagine, a reference to the current Labour administration, but a comment about the 1946 administration made in a report of the Royal Institute of Public Administration published in 1965.[1] The issue of how, when and where the government should or does communicate has been the subject of debate for almost as long as the Civil Service Commission has existed. The challenges for government communication in the modern environment – particularly in the context of broader trends in society and in the media – are more exacting now than they have ever been. This is the backdrop for expanding the remit of government communication, while reinforcing its underlying principles of political impartiality and honesty.

Modern times

We live in a world of media plenty – hundreds of channels and outlets, constant noise levels, a media hungry for news. More sources of information are accessible than ever before and faster than ever before. We are a networked society – both physically and in our behaviour. News can flash around a group of friends by text message as fast as it can flash around the world by e-mail. News can be watched as it happens – the impact of the attacks on the World Trade Center and the Pentagon were amplified by the horror of watching the plane crash into the second tower live on television. Media reports of the tsunami hitting in South-East Asia were instrumental in alerting governments and aid agencies to the scale of the tragedy as well as harnessing the sympathies and support of people across the world. Wars are now played out live to audiences around the globe, and the battle to capture the media high ground can be as intense as the battles for territory.

The world moves fast. There is a pervasive desire to innovate and to replace yesterday's favourites with something new. We are no longer content with mass produced, standardised goods and services but expect specialisation and customisation to fit personal needs. Increasingly citizens expect to be engaged in a dialogue with the institutions which touch our lives, in the same way as customers of retailers, supermarkets and airlines. They compete for loyalty and give rewards when we bestow it upon them, personalising the offers they make and capturing information each time we shop or travel.

Disillusionment with political process

Experience of commercial companies is now fuelling expectations of dealings with the state. We have begun to flex our consumer muscles, and rather enjoy the power. In contrast, research shows that we feel alienated and detached from the political process, with the malaise most apparent amongst younger votes. In the 2001 general election, voting fell to 59%, its lowest recorded level since 1919. Work carried out by the Prime Minister's Strategy Unit suggests various contributory factors – some due to the changing nature of the relationship between government and citizens and some down to deeper changes of values.

We have become more questioning of government's motives, with fewer people trusting government to put the national interest above party interest. Many talk of politicians becoming 'out of touch' particularly when elections are not in sight. Research published in 2004 by the Committee on Standards in Public Life[2] showed that respondents had low levels of trust in politicians generally (27%) but much higher levels of trust in their local MP (47%) and still more trust in their local police officers, head teachers and judges (75% or more). Personal familiarity and direct contact are important components of trust, but this does not offset the broader diminution of trust across the board, with only 35% of us agreeing that 'other people can be trusted' compared to almost 60% in 1959.

These trends are no doubt linked to becoming a less reverential society. We expect to be listened to but don't regard failing to vote as a dereliction of duty in the same way as the post-war generation. The loss of deference for traditional forms of authority – the monarchy, parliament, the armed forces and the church – is well charted.

But while deference declines, expectations continue to grow. We demand honesty, trustworthiness, and the ability to own up to and learn from mistakes from public institutions, while still expecting them to have the public interest at their heart. This is matched by a more "rights-based" public culture, underpinned by the Human Rights Act, the rise of ombudsmen, the Freedom of Information Act and evidenced by the increasing propensity to use litigation to resolve disputes and settle grievances.

It could therefore be argued that the values and traditions of the civil service as established 150 years ago with the formation of the Civil Service Commission are perfectly in tune with modern society, based as they are on serving the public and doing so with honesty, openness, impartiality and fairness. Indeed, the MORI trust scores for the civil service (percentage agreeing that civil servants could be trusted to tell the truth) compare favourably with those of both journalists and politicians and have doubled to around 50% over the past twenty years.[3] But if the public broadly trusts the civil service there is less clarity about the role that civil servants should play in communication and while much of the public debate on this issue appears to have taken place since 1997, when the change of government was accompanied by a more marked change in style, the subject is by no means a new one.

Birth of government communication

The first dedicated publicity unit within the Post Office (then a government department) was set up shortly after the birth of the modern civil service in the 1850s, in order to "bring the activities of the Post Office to public and Parliamentary notice." Its first wide-scale publicity campaign was carried out in 1876, when a million handbills were issued to alert the public to the virtues of government savings schemes, life insurance and annuities.

In 1926, the first power play between government and the newly incorporated BBC was in response to the General Strike which removed newspapers from the streets. The BBC refused to become a government mouthpiece, establishing a precedence that, despite regular skirmishes between them, has lasted nearly 80 years. The government's response in 1926 was to produce the first (and last!) government newspaper, the British Gazette.

The legitimacy of government communication was cemented in the 1930s; this is in no small part attributable to the skills and vision of Stephen Tallents, a civil servant from the Empire Marketing Board responsible for marketing British industry to the rest of the world. He argued that "The skilled and judicial employment of publicity is, I am convinced, a subject of major importance in public administration. It enjoys at present some lip service but little sound thought or practical experiment. It demands the most careful study and experiment and the application to both of first class brains and first class taste. Central government and local government must be weaned from the idea that publicity is a luxury, if not a folly. Publicity should be recognised as a professional job demanding special training and special capacities, which incidentally do not include a flair for personal boosting but do include in the broadest sense artistic capacity."[4]

Following a short-lived attempt in 1918, the second Ministry of Information was set up in 1939, tasked with mobilising public opinion and information to help the war effort. The Minister for Information was responsible in parliament for general government information policy, but the departmental ministers retained control over their own information policy. In the service of information and explanation, the Ministry of Information used every technique of publicity then available – films and broadcasting, press advertisements, posters, exhibitions, illustrated booklets and public lectures. They recruited writers and publicists from a wide variety of different backgrounds and set up a series of local information committees to collect and report on the views of the public. During the war, the government, for the first time, carried out national research to find out about the conditions in which people were living, and also to check on morale and the impact of government advertising.

The influence of the ministry alarmed some opposition MPs who felt that the increasing employment by government of people skilled in publicity matters could provide an advantage to the incumbent party that was not available to government's political opponents. There was also a concern that this growth in direct communication between government and the public would undermine the role of parliament, raising the spectre of government mobilising public support for its policies before parliament had had an opportunity to debate them! There was further criticism that information officers, paid for by the public, might become the personal property of their minister, provoked by several ministers who insisted on transferring their publicity officers when they moved departments

Civil service establishment

Following the war, the Ministry for Information was, once more, disbanded, but the role of the information officer was confirmed by the report of a Treasury Committee chaired by Sir James Crombie, which defined the role as being to "create and maintain an informed public opinion".[5] There was broad agreement that government has a right to be heard by and a duty to explain its activities to the public at large. However, a second committee, chaired by Sir Henry French, felt the spending levels were too high (an estimated £5 million was spent in 1949/50), and recommended that more use be made of the free media. Not unlike the Phillis Committee's recommendations,[6] over fifty years later, Sir Henry's group suggested that the government had become too reliant on one form of communication – in this case paid-for publicity – and recommended that "particular attention be paid to the correct choice and use of the various publicity media available".[7] As the mass media recovered in the post war period, much more government information could be put across as editorial, and the budget for paid-for material was reduced significantly.

In the immediate post-war period, the focus for government communication was the national press, which reported the activities of ministers and their departments and faithfully replayed parliamentary debates. The new medium of television initially made little difference to the style and nature of reporting, constrained as it was by the 14-Day Rule, introduced during the Second World War. This was an emergency measure prohibiting broadcast debate of any matter to be debated in parliament in the following fortnight. It effectively prohibited any topical political discussion on television and delayed the development of the medium as a way of challenging the government and its policies until the 1950s. The 1959 election was the first to be covered on television and Labour's press conference in 1964 was the first to be televised.

Key governmental and political roles

Since the war, two significant offices have shaped the governmental approach to communications – the Press Office at No 10 and the Minister for Information. Only one full time Minister for Information was ever appointed – William (later Lord) Deedes – a lobby journalist and war correspondent who became MP for Ashford between 1950 and 1974. From 1962 to 1964, as Minister for Information, his brief was to drum up enthusiasm and support for Britain's proposed entry into the then Common Market. As a minister, he answered questions in the House and participated in debates, as well as co-ordinating departmental press officers and keeping Conservative Central Office briefed on government publicity plans. He regarded the distinction between information and propaganda as both clear and important and was careful to stay on the right side, "We were very strict about the offside rule!"[8]. He went on to edit the *Daily Telegraph* between 1974 and 1986, and expressed the relationship between the press and the government at the time in a way that both parties may find familiar today – "When I was in Cabinet, I despaired of keeping anything secret. When I was an editor, I thought there must be masses of secrets being kept from me!"[9]

All Prime Ministers since the war have had their own adviser on communications at No 10. Some, such as Sir Anthony Eden, have appointed outsiders – he chose William Clark, a former *Observer* journalist. Joe Haines was a Lobby correspondent before working for Harold Wilson, and Alistair Campbell, Tony Blair's former Director of Communications, was a political journalist. Others have selected a civil servant to fill the role – Edward Heath chose a Foreign Office official and Bernard Ingham, who worked for Mrs Thatcher, was a civil servant with a background in journalism. When the role of Minister for Information was abandoned in the mid 1960s, the role of Chief Press Secretary at No 10 became the de facto lead for co-ordination and management of government communication.

Indeed it is Bernard Ingham who is largely attributed with the next phase of modernising government communications. Between 1979 and 1990, as Chief Press Secretary, he briefed the lobby with a mixture of on and off-the-record briefings and, as Head of the Government Information Service, chaired the meetings of government information officers to ensure that Mrs Thatcher's policies were put over with clarity and enthusiasm. As well as a clearer co-ordinating focus he saw his role as going beyond the mere provision of information, "Governments identify a need to communicate 'bad' news as well as good news, if only to put the best possible face on it."[10]

Era of rebuttal

The more complicated contours of the communication landscape caused both structural and attitudinal changes within government. The expansion of television, from one BBC channel to include first ITV, then BBC 2 and Channel 4 and finally cable and satellite multi-channel services, alongside the growth of red-topped daily papers, was to sweep away the gentler era of *Today in Parliament* and lengthy pages of parliamentary proceedings. Gallery reporting was largely overtaken by lobby journalism, with just the parliamentary sketch surviving in most newspapers.

This more competitive media market has, over time, driven harder reporting styles and strengthened the fourth estate's determination to hold the government of the day to account. The response of politicians was to sharpen up their media handling skills and treat the media more vigorously in return – the era of rebuttal was upon us. Those media handling skills were evident in the approach Margaret Thatcher took to her media appearances, using Gordon Reece – a former television producer – as her personal media adviser. He not only chose which programmes she would appear on, but also helped her with her style and appearance and the way she spoke, using opinion polls to inform his decisions. She also chose Saatchi and Saatchi to mastermind her election campaigns, introducing modern commercial marketing techniques to the political arena.

The expectations of the Labour Party when it came into power in 1997 had been shaped by its opposition years, when it developed a sophisticated and well-planned approach to media management. It believed that the political views of the public were predominantly shaped by the daily news and political reporting and this led to a clear political communication strategy that involved the careful wooing of daily newspapers and broadcasters as well as vigorous and tailored briefing of its candidates and MPs to ensure a clear and consistent message was conveyed.

With political parties professionalising their approach to the media, Sir Robin Mountfield's[11] report on the Government Information Service in 1997, reinforced the importance of political impartiality for government communication, while acknowledging the need to step up operations to cope with the 24-hour media world. New ministers also built up the use of special advisers to brief the media on political or personal matters where it would be inappropriate for civil servants to comment, causing comment about the number and authority of such advisers, not least because of the executive powers given to the Prime Minister's Director of Communication, himself a special adviser.

While the debate about special advisers, particularly those specialising in communication, was not a new one, it was at this time that the words 'spin' and 'spin-doctor' entered the public's consciousness. The now infamous events in the then Department for Transport, Local Government and the Regions in 2001 (when a special adviser, Jo Moore, was caught up in an argument with the department's Director of Communications, Martin Sixsmith) were to bring yet sharper focus to the issue with the Public Administration Select Committee's subsequent report into 'These Unfortunate Events' calling for a 'radical review of government communications'.

The subsequent Phillis Review recommended that the post of Director of Communications, then held by Alastair Campbell, should be split into two roles. One would continue to be a special adviser, focused on the Prime Minister's communication strategy, but without executive powers. The second role, a senior civil servant, would act as a Head of Profession for all those working in government communication and foster a wider remit for government communication, balancing the shorter-term media focus at No.10. This would also embed a clearer separation between political communication and government communication at the highest level.

Wider remit for government communication

By a wider remit for government communication Phillis intended an approach that, while firmly based on the traditional values of the civil service, would be one able to address the formidable challenges of the 21st century. Media reports of government and politics are dominated by personalities – often to the detriment of clear debate on policies. This makes the line between legitimate government communication and inappropriate political comment difficult for some to discern, and places even greater significance on the need for political impartiality in government communication and clear structures to support that.

The trend of public disengagement from the formal mechanisms of democracy persists and the public, particularly the young, now often prefer to express their views through individual action and around specific single issues. For government communicators this mean seeking new and innovative ways of engaging the public in debate and listening carefully to the ways in which views are being expressed. Stephen Coleman[12] has referred to this as being 'more radar and less loudhailer'.

We live in an age where governments need to do more than simply introduce legislation to enact their policies – successful government involves both persuading the public and professional communities of the need for legislation and engaging them in the process of developing the laws and processes that will deliver on their expectations. This means communication needs to be built into the policy process from conception to implementation defining a wider and more ambitious remit for government communication in the 21st century, but one which retains core civil service values of honesty and impartiality. The Government Communication Network set up in 2004, embracing all those working within communications and including the full range of professional skills, is the first step in delivering this broader remit.

It will enable government to understand and respond to the extraordinary growth in new communication channels such as e-mail and text messaging and use these channels to build new connections between government and those it governs. Within this wider remit, however, traditional skills have to be maintained, especially media relations. Despite falling ratings and newspaper circulations, daily skirmishes between politicians and political correspondents are still much in evidence, and no government will wish the political or social preferences of the national dailies to dictate an agenda, arguing that politicians, supported by an electoral mandate, should lead public debate.

Voice of the public

Government communication should have two overriding objectives: to make the voice of the public heard at the policy table so that government develops and delivers services which better reflect people's expectations and desires; and to improve the public's awareness and understanding of government policies and actions so that people can more readily identify and access information and services relevant to their daily lives.

We need to more fully embrace a culture of explanation – where communication informs all stages of the policy making process. The government already consults the public and stakeholders through its pre-legislative consultation processes, but this needs to be extended and new and innovative ways need to be found to reach out and listen to people – particularly those currently turned off by government and politics. If the views and reactions of the public and other stakeholders are listened to and communicated in ways that are trusted and appropriate for each group there are two prizes. Firstly, improved policy and services and, secondly, the potential to re-engage people in the democratic process.

People are generally most interested in government when it affects them personally and in their own communities. They are interested in their local school, their local hospital, crime in their area, and less so in national statistics and performance. The public want to be involved, but on their own terms. They trust local media, television, radio and press more than they do the national media. More communication effort and resource needs to be focused on interpreting national policy into what it means for people locally, and a wider range of communication channels need to be used to have a better chance of engaging people.

The public do not think in departmental terms but look to government as a whole for information. Developing cross-governmental communications, such as direct.gov.uk, will help to provide information in a way that users find easy and intuitive to browse and search.

But if the emphasis is being broadened the heritage of the values should not change. If there is to be a common currency for debate, for information shared and trusted by the public, the media and the political classes, the impartiality of the civil service will need to continue to underpin all government communication activity. In the words of a former No 10 Press Officer, "the tools will change, but the ethos should remain the same."[13]

The Civil Service Commissioners have an important role to play now, as they have done in the past. Since the role of information officer was first created in 1946, the profession of communications has been part of the Civil Service Commissioners' remit, ensuring that high standards are maintained in recruitment, whether the candidates be internal or external. In the face of the pressures and temptations that characterise the current engagement between the media, the government and the public, few would disagree that the principles of the civil service are as necessary now as they have ever been.

Notes

1. *The Government Explains* by Marjorie Ogilvy-Webb, George Allen and Unwin Ltd, 1965

2. Survey of Public Attitudes towards Conduct in Public Life, BMRB Social Research for the Committee on Standards in Public Life September 2004

3. MORI Research into Opinion of Professions 1983–2004

4. Sir Stephen Tallents *Salesmanship in the Public Service: Scope and Technique* Public Administration Vol XI, July 1933

5. The report of the Crombie Committee was not published, but it was issued as an annex to a Treasury instruction, Establishments Circular 5/45, August 1949

6. An Independent Review of Government Communications, presented to the Minister for the Cabinet Office, January 2004

7. Report of the Committee on the cost of the Home Information Services Cms. 7836, HMSO, 1949

8. Author's interview with Lord Deedes, February 2005

9. Author's interview with Lord Deedes, February 2005

10. Bernard Ingham quoted in *Sources Close to the Prime Minister*, Cockerell, Hennessy and Walker, Macmillan 1984

11. Sir Robin Mountfield was then a Permanent Secretary in the Cabinet Office

12. Evidence given to the Phillis Review of Government Communication 2003

13. Interview with the author, February 2005

CHANGING **TIMES**

An International Perspective on Government Efficiency in a Democracy

Elaine Kamarck looks at public sector reform movements around the world, arguing that what began as a desire for better efficiency and lower costs has brought about a new appreciation for quality and performance. As government presides over an increasingly sophisticated economy, a culture of innovation and the need to attract top talent becomes paramount.

Elaine Kamarck

Elaine C. Kamarck is a Lecturer in Public Policy who came to the Kennedy School in 1997 after a career in politics and government. In the 1980s, she was one of the founders of the New Democrat movement which helped elect Bill Clinton president.

She served in the White House from 1993 to 1997, where she created and managed the Clinton Administration's National Performance Review, also known as reinventing government. At the Kennedy School she served as Director of Visions of Governance for the Twenty-First Century and as Faculty Advisor to the Innovations in American Government Awards Program.

In 2000, she took a leave of absence to work as senior policy advisor to the Gore campaign. She conducts research on 21st century government, the role of the internet in political campaigns, homeland defence, intelligence reorganisation, and governmental reform and innovation. Kamarck received her PhD in political science from the University of California, Berkeley.

Government in the Information Age

Background to the global government reform movement.

The twentieth century was the bureaucratic century. In the public sector and in the private sector the dominant organisational form was the large, hierarchical, rule bound entity known as bureaucracy. In the private sector bureaucracy was the organisational analogue to the assembly line and the scientific management revolution started by Frederick Taylor. And, as so often happens, the public sector followed suit, creating hierarchical organisations that broke down complex tasks into definable and discrete sub tasks and then broke those tasks down into smaller sub tasks and so on. By mid century, in America and in most developed countries, the organisational structures of the private sector and the pubic sector were similar.

But by the end of the twentieth century the private sector was changing and those changes were affecting the way citizens saw their government. Contrast, for example, the experience of going to the bank in 1954, with the experience of going to the bank in 1994. In 1954 you had to go to a bank between 9:00 in the morning and 3:00 in the afternoon (banker's hours). You had to stand in line, see a teller, and have your documents ready. If you were lucky the teller was nice. (If your bank had a monopoly in town, your teller didn't really have much incentive to be nice.) Basically, however, doing business in the private sector circa 1954 was not much different than doing business in the public sector such as going to get a passport or a driver's licence. The organisations operated in similar ways.

Now fast forward to 1994. The information revolution allowed banks to replace most tellers with ATM machines and eventually home-based internet banking. People complained about the impersonality of this – for about two seconds. And then they quickly became accustomed to the ease and the convenience of banking any time they wanted to – day or night. As in so many other areas of the consumer world, convenience to the customer became a key to organisational success and to organisational re-structuring.

But this was not so in government. In the public sector in 1994 you still had to go to an office, stand in line and hope that if you got to the end of the line before the office closed you had the right information with you and could in fact complete your business. In 1954 that didn't infuriate people as much as it did in 1994. For by 1994 the private sector was changing and the public sector was not.

Citizens noticed and complained. Typical of the letters that used to come into the National Performance Review Office in the Clinton/Gore White House was one from Los Angeles.[1] The letter was from an obviously well to do man, since the first thing he told us was that in the previous year he had paid over $400,000 in federal income taxes. That, however, was not what had made him mad enough to write to us. He had gone to the passport office to get his newborn daughter a passport. He had stood in line for a very long time and then the office had simply closed and told him to come back the next day. That really made him mad.

In the waning decades of the twentieth century, the new organisational forms and capacities of the information age began to replace the organisational forms of the industrial age. Citizens of first world countries, accustomed to a high level of responsiveness from the private sector, experienced frustration and eventually a lack of confidence in the bureaucratic state. In America and in other parts of the world, bureaucracy itself – seen as expensive, inflexible, unfriendly, frequently incompetent – became the enemy – above and beyond the public purposes to which it was dedicated. President Clinton often told about working a rope line during the health care debates in his first term and coming upon a woman who pressed his hand, looked into his eyes and urged him, with great passion, to make sure "that the government keeps its hands off my Medicare."[2]

Thus policy makers at the beginning of the twenty-first century face the following conundrum – how do you govern in an era when people hate the government? What do you do when the public tells people in government "Fix this now!" but adds "Oh, and by the way, don't let the government do it." This sentiment is indicative of failure – not in the purposes of government but in the means of government – and the dominant means of government in the twentieth century has been bureaucracy. Democracies are so accustomed to arguing about the proper scope and purpose of government that they have had a hard time recognising that much of the current debate over government is not over what it does but how it does it.

And yet a focus on the "how" instead of the "what" of government has occurred in national capitals all over the world. It has created a global or international language about government reform and efficiency. This global government reform movement has had two distinct but overlapping phases. Stage one took place primarily during the 1980s. In that decade governments concentrated on economic liberalisation and on privatising industries that had previously been state owned. For instance, in Latin America this first stage was primarily concerned with privatisation of state-owned enterprises and removing the "heavy hand" of the state from the economy. Many of the newly emerging democracies in the former Soviet bloc are still involved, to a greater or lesser extent, in the privatisation of state owned industries and, at the beginning of the twenty-first century even China has begun a gradual privatisation of its huge state owned industries.

The United States, however, was an exception to this first stage. According to Graham Scott, former Treasury Secretary of New Zealand, for most of the world the first stage of governmental reform revolved primarily around getting government out of businesses such as airlines, telephones etc. that the United States was never in to begin with. "The United States was never really trying to solve the problem that most of the rest of us began with," said Scott at the Global Forum on Reinventing Government held in Washington in January of 1999. While Ronald Reagan shared Margaret Thatcher's anti-bureaucratic rhetoric he never had the targets that Thatcher and other national leaders had for privatisation and hence privatised very little. In sum, the first stage of government reform should be seen in the context of the transition to free market economies that began all over the world in the 1980s and accelerated in 1989 with the fall of the Berlin Wall.

The second decade of this movement – beginning in the 1990s – focused less on privatisation per se and more on the administrative reform of core state functions and the building of state capacity. In this decade states have sought to cut the size of their governmental bureaucracies while simultaneously making government more efficient, more modern, more responsive to the citizen and less corrupt. In the decade of the 1990s, the United States, under President Clinton and his Vice President, Al Gore, undertook to "reinvent" government and thus added its own unique approach to the governmental reform movements that were already underway in many other countries. While first world countries concentrated on efficiency and the extensive introduction of information technology into government, developing countries concentrated on building state capacity, decentralisation and fighting corruption.[3]

As the pace of governmental reform picked up – fueled by widespread public distrust of government in the United States, the requirements of the Maastricht Treaty in Europe, the demands of major lending institutions such as the World Bank and the IMF in developing countries and the democratisation of many previously communist countries – concepts dealing with governmental efficiency and public administration reform spread rapidly from one country to another – often without even a change in the terminology.[4] In the introduction to a volume on public sector management in Europe, the editors state: "In some reports we found that the language had not even been translated from the American to the local language."[5] And in other instances, the terms were mixed. For instance, the Westminster countries adopted Citizen's Charters in order to improve service delivery; the Americans adopted Customer Service. In several countries the term Customer Charters is used.

Common aspects of the global reform agenda

While many of the reform movements around the world began with a rather simple and straightforward desire for better efficiency and lower costs – they have been accompanied by a new appreciation for quality and performance in government. The disintegration of the former Soviet Union into countries with tenuous attachments to the rule of law, the continuing saga of poverty and desperation in African states with barely functioning governments, and a new, post 9/11 understanding of the security dangers posed by failed states such as Afghanistan – have reminded many people that, even in a time of borderless economies and international markets, effective functioning states are still the primary prerequisites for successful societies.

Against this backdrop reform has taken place in most countries in one or more of the following six areas:

- reducing the cost of government;
- improving the quality of government services;
- fostering a civil service for the 21st century;
- making use of information technology;
- balancing regulation with the need for economic efficiency;
- creating honest and transparent government.

Strong financial controls and an effective budget process are essential for governments seeking to reduce costs and keep spending under control. As nations around the world have sought to reduce government spending in order to stimulate a stronger private sector and higher direct foreign investment, they have turned to a variety of budget innovations.

Perhaps the most profound change in government budgeting has been the introduction of productivity as a concept relevant to government expenditures. Productivity is not a term commonly associated with government and yet, in the past two decades, many of the budget and financial reforms have, at their root, the goal of measuring productivity and establishing it as a concept around which to budget. Several interrelated strategies have emerged to enhance productivity thus helping government cost less. They are:

- cost accounting;
- performance based budgeting;
- flexibility among budget accounts;
- capturing savings for the organisation;
- promoting innovation and productivity.

The assumption implicit in these new budgeting strategies is that organisational productivity will increase as goals are clearly articulated and traditional line item budgeting is dropped, allowing for more creativity and innovation. Increasingly governments have stopped micro-managing agency budgets and have started to allow agencies to move money between accounts as needed to achieve the organisation's goals.

Finally, many countries realise that in order to promote productivity they must create a system that will allow for constant innovation. And, as many studies of organisations – both public and private – have shown, innovation tends to come, not from the top people in the organisation but from those in the middle and on the front lines.[6] Thus the best public sector organisations tend to create an atmosphere in which all employees – from top to bottom – feel free to participate and to communicate about saving money and improving performance.

For most governments, most of the time, the primary cost of government, after payments to citizens, is the wage bill. But cutting the wage bill is difficult and controversial. In many countries, government employment has been used as a means of reducing social tension and substituting for a weak private sector economy. For instance, for many years some African nations promised government employment to their university graduates in order to keep their most educated people in country. Yet pressure from the major lending institutions to bring budget deficits down has led to significant downsizing in governments around the world in the last twenty years – ending a period of growth in government employment that had begun to slow in the early 1970s.

So how big should government be? There is no right answer to this question. Rather, the question every country needs to ask itself is – How productive is the government that we have and should we limit or eliminate government activities that are less productive? Insights on the question of the proper size of government come out of the work of Donald Rowat.[7] Contrary to conventional wisdom, Rowat found that OECD countries typically have higher levels of employment in general government than do developing countries. He then looked at the distribution of the government work force and found that the OECD countries typically have larger numbers of people working for state and local government than do the developing countries. Developing countries typically have larger numbers of people working for central government.

The implications of these general tendencies are important. Local government workers tend to be teachers, public health nurses and police – people who are actually involved in creating a stronger and safer community. Central government employment tends to be more involved with bureaucratic processing. Thus the wage bill itself can be large or small, the real issue is – are the people who work for the government involved in activities that contribute to productivity in the general population? Governments need to be involved in "right-sizing" public employment.

Nonetheless, countries in financial crisis often have to downsize without the benefit of first figuring out what their "right size" is. In doing so they have adopted many strategies for reducing their government's wage bill. They have:

- frozen or reduced wages;
- frozen recruitment;
- engaged in programs to get rid of "ghost workers" (workers who get paid but don't work);
- eliminated automated entry into the civil service upon completion of university;
- eliminated automatic promotions;
- introduced voluntary redundancies by offering people money to leave

government employment;

- introduced compulsory redundancies – let workers go with little or no money;
- offered early retirement packages in order to induce older workers to leave government employment;
- and they have privatised.

When it comes to reducing the cost of government by downsizing as many lessons have been learned in what not to do as in what to do. In many instances, the capacity of the private sector to absorb new workers is low and these strategies then go on to create other problems for the economy. In some developing countries one government worker in a central city may be supporting many other family members in the countryside. Voluntary redundancy programmes in which workers are paid to leave government employment often result in the youngest and most qualified workers leaving because they can most easily find employment in the private sector. Thus if governments are not careful about how they structure these programmes they can result in a severe "brain drain." "Ghost workers" have been known to return to the government payroll if inadequate control mechanisms are not put in place following the initial audit.

But the picture is not all bad. Successful downsizing usually involves two key principles. First, if at all possible, government downsizing should be done as a routine, gradual affair during periods of relatively low unemployment in the private sector. And second, government downsizing should seek to re-distribute government jobs from central cities to the states and localities and from bureaucratic work to front line work that builds capacity in the population. Under President Bill Clinton and Vice President Al Gore, the United States government cut its workforce by over 17% – exceeding everyone's expectations. However, since the U.S. reform movement was motivated more by a confidence crisis than an economic crisis, much of this downsizing took place under generally favorable economic conditions. Using a combination of buy-outs (voluntary redundancies) and attrition (deciding not to fill vacant positions) some government agencies shrunk by as much as 20%. In addition, President Clinton used the savings from personnel reduction to place more policemen on the streets thus furthering the goal of reducing crime.

Improving the quality of government services is critical to restoring and maintaining trust in government whether that government is in Western Europe, China or Africa. In post-apartheid South Africa service delivery became a critical area to the transformation of government. An early white paper on service delivery was called "Batho Pele," a Sesotho adage meaning "People First." And in China, improvements in service delivery are part and parcel of the Communist Party's desire to modernise the economy and create satisfaction with government (thus preventing multi-party democracy.)

But for all governments around the world the government of Great Britain has served as a model of service delivery with the development of the Citizen's Charter and subsequent innovations in "joined up" government. In the United States, the federal government adopted Customer Service Standards but throughout most of the world the Citizen's Charter concept is copied – in executive and in name.

As governments around the world have sought to improve service delivery they have adopted one or more of the following strategies. They have:

- set up "one-stop shops" or places where a person, usually a business owner, can conduct all their transactions with the government at once,
- attempted to find out from citizens what they want and expect from government services;
- allowed citizen inputs to shape bureaucratic organisation and behaviour;
- disseminated to the public standards for the organisation to reach;
- measured performance and published whether or not the standards were met;
- involved employees in the redesign of the organisation;
- trained government employees in customer service and organised internal incentives around the accomplishment of quality standards.

True quality in service delivery, however, cannot be implemented without a degree of democracy since all of the above rely heavily on free participation and input from citizens. In a study of World Bank projects, Daniel Kaufmann and Lant H. Pritchett found that projects in countries where there was a degree of democracy and transparency were more likely to be successful than projects in countries with lower levels of democracy.[8] In addition, improving service often requires resources that poor governments do not have.

At the beginning of the twenty-first century most governments around the world find that they are confronting one or more of the following problems as they try to maintain a workforce commensurate to the challenges of government. In developed countries the public sector has trouble competing with the private sector where wages at the top tend to be much higher, while developing countries, especially in Africa, have trouble competing with NGOs where wages are funded with western money and tend to be higher. In developed countries decades of tight budgets has meant that money for training is often cut first and yet most governments face a need for highly skilled labour. Public sector employees face wage compression (those at the top arc not paid much more than those at the bottom) and this causes talented executives to leave public service. Countries with a long-standing civil service tradition find that they have to fight excessive rules and regulations which often make jobs inflexible and rewards difficult. In contrast, many developing countries and new democracies struggle with excessive political patronage that regularly undercuts merit principles and results in a high turnover of government employees. And finally, in all too many countries, public servants do not operate under the rule of law.

In order to improve the quality of their public sector workforce countries are:
- attempting to reduce wage disparities between the public and private (or NGO) sectors;
- attempting to reduce pay compression in the civil service;
- reforming obsolete civil service rules and regulations;
- instituting performance based pay systems;

- targeting scarce skills and opening up the system to new talent and to diverse people;
- balancing the need for a stable, merit based system with the need for political direction in the government.

The information revolution is creating the ability to transform bureaucratic government. Digital government has the power to reduce the cost of government, increase citizen input into government, improve official decision-making and increase the transparency of government transactions. Most governments in the world now have web pages. In very poor countries those web pages are clearly designed exclusively for Americans and Western Europeans, offering information on trade and tourism. However, in some more developed countries such as Mexico, are using the web to implement programs such as "Compranet" to increase the transparency of government contracts and awards in an effort to combat corruption and cronyism.

But in most first world countries government web pages seek to facilitate transactions between citizens and their governments. Most first world countries now allow for some or all tax filings on line and in spite of some well publicised problems this trend is likely to continue well into the future with considerable cost savings to government as clerks and store fronts are gradually replaced by the internet.[9] This, however, will only exacerbate the need for highly trained information technologists to run the government of the 21st century.

In addition to serving the citizen and defending the country, regulating the private sector is one of the most important functions of government. For some developing countries the challenge is to create a regulatory structure that is honest and reliable. Sound regulatory policy cannot happen without the rule of law and therefore, for many developing countries, regulatory reform must go hand in hand with efforts to reform the judicial system. Other developing countries find themselves having to create regulatory systems to oversee newly privatised sectors of the economy. And all countries find that they need to have some process for calculating the cost of regulations, lest regulations become an undue burden on a developing economy.

Calculating the regulatory burden on an economy is perhaps the first step in creating effective regulation. As Giandomenico Majone points out, "The public budget is a soft constraint on regulators because the real costs of regulatory programs are borne not by the agencies producing the regulations but by the individuals and firms who have to comply with the regulations. These costs remain hidden because they do not appear in the budget. The most important regulatory reform consists in calculating (and making public) such costs."[10]

Regulatory reform is a critical, if imperfectly understood aspect of economic development. The greater the regulatory hurdle the larger the disincentive to entrepreneurship. In parts of the developing world dense and antiquated regulatory systems drive entrepreneurship underground to the "informal" sector of the economy. And as many have written, the existence of a large "informal" economy ultimately works against the talented poor entrepreneurs since they are not able to establish property rights, they are not able to accumulate capital and they are not able to pass on their accumulated money to their children – thus creating new generations of poverty.[11]

In the developed world, decades of regulation often serve to create enormous burdens on entrepreneurship, resulting in calls for the simplification of regulations. Nowhere is this more evident than in the evolution of the European Union. As they become one economic unit, EU regulations have been passed on top of already existing national regulations.

The most common strategies adopted for balancing regulation with economic efficiency have been to:

- assess cost;
- simplify regulations and/or reduce the number of regulations;
- consult with affected parties in the creation of legislation and regulation.

There is a profound moral imperative behind the need to fight corruption. But in addition to the powerful moral imperative to fighting corruption there has been added, in recent years, a powerful economic imperative. To put it simply, countries with high levels of corruption tend to be poor and to remain poor. Why is that? According to Brian Jenkins of Kroll Associates $350 billion of foreign aid is estimated to be in Swiss bank accounts – a significant factor in "donor fatigue."[12] Second, with the end of the Cold War, the ratio of public to private sector capital flows to emerging and developing countries changed dramatically. According to two IMF economists, at the beginning of the 1990s the amount of private capital flows to emerging and developing countries was about the same as the amount of public capital flows. But by the end of that decade and the beginning of the 21st century, private capital flows had substantially outstripped public capital flows by a factor of six.[13]

The emergence of large private sector capital flows meant that countries with low levels of corruption, rule of law, protection of property rights and effective and honest regulatory structures were favoured in terms of Foreign Direct Investment. Another IMF economist, Paolo Mauro studied 106 countries and found that one standard deviation in the "corruption index" is associated with a more than 4% increase in the investment rate and more than half a percentage point increase in annual growth rate per Gross Domestic Product.[14] Moreover, the same economist showed that increases in corruption tended to lower the rate of public spending on education – a disaster for countries trying to grow into industrial and information age economies.[15]

For many years the developed world was complicit in perpetuating corruption in the developing world, looking upon it as a "cost of business" and allowing, in some countries, bribes to be deducted as business expenses. But in 1999 that changed. Recognizing that "…corruption exacts an inordinately high price on the poor by denying them access to vital basic services," the OECD led the way by introducing the Convention on Combating Bribery of Foreign Public Officials in International Business Transactions.[16] The purpose of the convention is to require that the more than 35 signatories to the convention make the bribing of a foreign public official a crime in their country and to implement systems to enforce the law. As Peter Eigen, whose group Transparency International was crucial to the success of this convention, points out, these 35 countries account for more than 90% of foreign direct investment worldwide.[17]

Thus the world's governments find themselves, at the beginning of the new century, dedicated to the reduction of official corruption. What do we know about this?

- Countries must create a truly transparent public sector.
- Countries must, in addition, create an "information culture" among their citizens so that citizens know they have a right to public sector information.
- The annual corruption rankings of Transparency International create international pressure on nations to try and reduce corruption.
- Countries must enforce the law and prosecute corrupt officials.
- But, countries must also look to the roots of corruption and engage in de-regulation and simplification of government processes if they are to get at the roots of corruption.
- In first world countries where levels of public corruption tend to be low, government officials have to find the right balance between fraud control on the one hand and productivity and service on the other.

In recent years, innovators like the former Mayor of LaPaz, Bolivia, Ronnie MacLean-Abaroa have shown why investigating and prosecuting public officials is not an adequate method for fighting corruption if the underlying systems are so complex and difficult that they breed corruption. When MacLean-Abaroa took over as Mayor, he discovered a comprehensive system of corruption. While he did prosecute corrupt officials he also set out to make the processes of government simpler and more transparent. When he began reforming the system there were over one hundred different taxes that citizens were required to pay, property taxes were meaningless, there was extensive over-regulation in permits and licensing, and extensive and systemic corruption in procurement. As part of his reforms he made government salaries comparable with the private sector, while cutting numbers and increasing the quality of employees. He reduced the procurement system from 26 steps to 6 steps and introduced competition and transparency into the system. He simplified taxes and cut the number of taxes from 126 to 7. Finally he simplified everything he could from building permits to health permits. The result? Revenues increased (along with international credit worthiness), corruption decreased and the Mayor was re-elected four times.[18]

Finally, governments in first world countries need to find the right balance between regulation and productivity. Large scale transfer payment programmes such as the Medicaid and Medicare programs in the Unites States are magnets for fraud and yet the traditional governmental response to fraud in those programmes has been to impose more regulations on providers – thus increasing cost without necessarily decreasing fraud. The title of one book on this topic says it all *The Pursuit of Absolute Integrity: How Corruption Control Makes Government Ineffective.*[19]

Looking forward

If the first generation of a global search for government efficiency consisted of privatising state run industrics and the second generation consists of strategies to advance the six goals discussed above – what will the third generation look like? A few closing thoughts on that topic.

We have only just begun to reap the productivity gains that are possible from the information revolution. Even the most sophisticated governments have to retain dual systems – web applications stand alongside old-fashioned store fronts. But with the passing of generations most government activities will move to the web – generating enormous savings to the government and generating enormous risks. So far the term "cyber-terrorism" is simply that – a term and not a reality. As government begins to live in cyberspace it will acquire an entirely new set of vulnerabilities.

Another challenge to government will be to move beyond websites and break down the organisational barriers that impede truly effective service delivery. But the real frontier is in using the internet to provide government with real time interactions between citizens and the civil service. This is a potentially deeper and more profound democratisation than that offered by periodic elections. Lip service is often given to this goal but only in Canada have officials attempted to use the internet to increase citizen input and improve official decision making.

As government presides over a more and more sophisticated economy it will need to attract top talent. That means making government salaries competitive with private sector salaries. Look to the government of Singapore for leadership in that area. There top government salaries are pegged to equivalent private sector salaries. This has been a key element in their successful fight against corruption. In the United States the government in the middle of the 20th century was a government of clerks. The US government by the middle of the 21st century needs to be a government of highly skilled integrators of complex systems. Getting there will involve some substantial political courage as elected officials lobby to close the growing gap between top public and private salaries.

As the world experiences more and more upheavals from weather related and disease related crises pressure will increase for greater environmental regulation and this will severely test the regulatory capacity of national governments and international institutions. As the environmentalists, Daniel Esty and Robert Mendelsohn point out, "…coal burning in China measurably affects Japan…water pollution in the Danube harms up to seven countries before the river empties into the Black Sea… As the world economy grows, transboundary pollution spillovers are likely to increase – rendering country-by-country responses ever more inadequate."[20] Regulatory policy has always been contentious within national borders, in the next century trans-national environmental regulation will pose as yet unimagined challenges.

Finally, governments will need to maintain and foster transparency in order to retain public confidence and be held accountable. Here is where democracy and sound public administration come together. While the world has made great strides in democratisation in the last three decades, that democratisation has often been incomplete. Elections have been held, power has changed hands peacefully but the routine interactions between citizens and their government are still governed by an unchanging ruling class that is all too often plagued by corruption, dishonesty and prejudice. The first world needs to protect the hard won independence and honesty of the civil service tradition and the rest of the world needs to create a civil service that can lead to more just societies.

Notes

1. The National Performance Review was a White House Office under the direction of Vice President Al Gore which was dedicated to "reinventing" the US Federal Government. It stayed in existence from 1993 to 2000. The author was Al Gore's senior policy advisor in charge of that initiative from 1993 to 1997.

2. Medicare is the United States Federal Government's health care program for the elderly.

3. However, these differences between reform movements are not absolute. Developing countries are also interested in efficiency and technology and first world countries are concerned about state capacity and corruption.

4. For instance, in Great Britain a programme begun to improve public service to the citizen is called The Citizen's Charter and in the United States the same programme is called Customer Service. At a 1996 UN General Assembly Session on Public Administration Reform countries referred to their own programmes using either the British or the American terms or sometimes by mixing those terms into Customer Charters or Citizens' Service.

5. Norman Flynn and Franz Stehl, editors, *Public Sector Management in Europe* (Hempstead, Prentice Hall Europe, 1996), p. 1.

6. Bill Bolton and John Thompson, *Entrepreneurs: Talent, Temperament, Technique*, Chapter 1 "Identifying the entrepreneur," pp. 11–47 and Sanford Borins, *Innovating with Integrity: How local heroes are transforming American government*, Chapter 3 "The Who, Why and How of Innovation," pp. 37–65.

7. Donald Rowat, "Comparing bureaucracies in developed and developing countries: a statistical analysis," *International Review of Public Sector Management*, (London, Sage Publications, Vol. 56 (1990), pp. 211-236.

8. "Civil Liberties, Democracy and the Performance of Government Projects", *The World Bank Economic Review*, Vol. 11, #2, May, 1997.

9. In the summer of 2002, the British government had to shut down its online tax filing system when it was discovered that citizens could read and even overwrite other people's tax returns on the site.

10. Paper presented at the Fifth Global Forum on Reinventing Government, Mexico City, November 3, 2003.

11. See the work of Hernando DeSoto.

12. "Corruption in the Global Marketplace", a presentation by Brian Michael Jenkins of Kroll Associates, April 30, 1997.

13. George T. Abed and Sanjeev Gupta, editors, *Governance, Corruption and Economic Performance*, (Washington, D.C., International Montary Fund, 9/23/02.)

14. "Corruption and Growth," *The Quarterly Journal of Economics*, Vol. #10, Issue #3, August, 1995, pp. 681–712.

15. See Paolo Mauro, George T. Abed and Sanjeev Gupta, editors, *Governance, Corruption and Economic Performance*, (Washington, D.C., International Montary Fund, 9/23/02.)

16. OECD Policy Brief, September 2000.

17. "The Need for sustained Efforts: recent anti-corruption reforms in Mexico," by Peter Eigen, prepared for the Fifth Global Forum on Reinventing Government, Mexico City, November 3, 2003.

18. Ronald Maclean-Abaroa, "Fighting Corruption in La Paz, Bolivia: A Case Study," presented to Dr. Kamarck's class, Spring, 1999.

19. By Frank Anechiarico and James B. Jacobs, (Chicago, University of Chicago Press, 1996.)

20. "Moving from National to International Environmental Policy," in *Policy Sciences*, Vol. 31, #3, 1998, pp. 225–235.

CHANGING **TIMES**

Index